| THIS |
| MUST | BE
| DOCUMENTED |

| THIS |
| MUST | BE
| DOCUMENTED |
Real Deliverance for the LGBTQ+D

Deon K. Williams

kenTell's Truth *Publishing*

THIS MUST BE DOCUMENTED: Real Deliverance for the LGBTQ+D.
Copyright © 2020 by Deon K. Williams.

All rights reserved. No part of this publication may be reproduced in any form, or by any means whatsoever; mechanical or electronic, including photocopying, recording, or of any information browsing, storage, or retrieval system, without written permission from the publisher, except for the use of appropriate citing's or brief quotations such as in the use of articles, reviews, or the likes! **Printed in the United States**. Publishing information and contact are as follows: kenTell's Truth Publishing, P.O. Box 77651, Atlanta, Georgia, 30357. (In association with SOUL FOOD INTERNATIONAL MINISTRIES, Inc.), www.SFIM.org |

Scriptures marked AMP are taken from the AMPLIFIED BIBLE (AMP): Scripture taken from the AMPLIFIED® BIBLE, Copyright © 1954, 1958, 1962, 1964, 1965, 1987 by the Lockman Foundation Used by Permission. (www.Lockman.org)

Scripture quotations are from the ESV® Bible (The Holy Bible, English Standard Version®), copyright © 2001 by Crossway, a publishing ministry of Good News Publishers. Used by permission. All rights reserved.

Scriptures marked KJV are taken from the KING JAMES VERSION (KJV): KING JAMES VERSION, public domain.

Author Photography: Domanie Barber; Jamaal Andrews | Cover Design: Haryolar Deeny

SECOND EDITION - **ISBN: 978-0-578-32617-7**

Although this publication is designed to provide accurate information regarding the subject matter of spiritual maturation of Christian and godly values, both parties of Publisher and the Author assume no responsibility for errors, inaccuracies, omissions, or any other considered inconsistencies within this publication. It is intended to serve as a source of valuable information; however, it is not meant to serve as a replacement for direct psychological or any other, sorts of expertise nor assistance. If such level of assistance is required, the services of a competent professional should be sought.

The Library of Congress has cataloged the paperback edition as follows:
[Print the CIP data for the original edition minus the standard CIP legend.]

Names: Williams, Deon K., author.
Title: This must be documented : real deliverance for the LGBTQ+D / Deon K. Williams.
Description: Atlanta, GA: kenTell's Truth Publishing, 2020.
Identifiers: LCCN: 2020925308 | ISBN: 978-0-578-83096-4
Subjects: LCSH Homosexuality--Religious aspects--Christianity. | Christian gays--Religious life. | Sex--Religious aspects--Christianity. | Sexual orientation--Religious aspects. | Sexual ethics--Religious aspects. | Homosexuality--Biblical teaching. | Christian ethics. | BISAC RELIGION / Christian Living / Family & Relationships | RELIGION / Christian Living / Personal Growth | RELIGION / Christian Living / Social Issues | SELF-HELP / Spiritual | SELF-HELP / Gender & Sexuality
Classification: LCC BR115.H6 .W55 2020 | DDC 261.8/35766--dc23

DEDICATION

This book is dedicated to those who have walked through life slightly confused, and uncertain about your identity; those who feel as if they've been ostracized by society for simply not being understood. Particularly if you were raised incorrectly in the church or Christian household.

-

There is a Right and Wrong way!

It's dedicated to every person, shamed, abandoned by your family; the disowned, and the likes! To those, scarred by the things said to you and the names you've been called.

-

Because words do hurt!

This book goes out to every person living in misery; being forced to marry because that's what you were told; thus, pretending to love persons forced upon you, that "God, didn't put together" to begin with. - And the list goes on, as it pertains to the psychological abuses, due to neurological fallout from high levels of toxicity, caused by certain erroneous teachings in the Body of Christ.

LASTLY.
This book is dedicated to the Church.
I hope you listen well.

I'd like to thank my God, whose name is **the LORD,** for entrusting me with this assignment. Father, I desire that You be pleased with me, and that You be glorified, and that Your Kingdom here on Earth be advanced. I'm praying for widespread help, to come from this project for many, and for many decades to come.

To *Pastor Carmelite (Lofton) Williams,*
Thank you for being very instrumental and as helpful, walking me through this process. – You are your brother's keeper! Thank you. Guys/gals; check out her material!
For your concern for Father's business, particularly, since that goes beyond what He's called just you to do, Thank you AGAIN.

To *SOUL FOOD INTERNATIONAL MINISTRIES, Inc.*, my Church family, WHO, at the time of the *first edition's* release, *didn't* know I had been working on this project, but thank you all for how you support me; making it possible to extend myself beyond 'the four walls' *so to speak*, and for the support of purchasing it when it was released. For the church's ministerial personnel who have stepped up, to make pastor's job a little lighter, to you I say: Every bit helps, and your support in servicing God's people *(with me)* has helped free me up enough to manifest this baby. Thank you.

#SFIMATL

I hope you all *are*, and *will* only *be* proud of me, for putting my life's reputation on the line, to sincerely help somebody else.

– for – those struggling unnecessarily, for not being cared for appropriately spiritually, and left to *die* (*in sin*), I GOT YOU!

To every person who reads this, THANK YOU.
All supporters of this project, present and future-tense, and lovers of truth (anyhow), and those who might advertise this literary piece by word of mouth; please do. May the content inside be worth that to you, *that you do so!* Thank you also as well.

TABLE OF CONTENTS

i.	DEDICATION	v
ii.	ACKNOWLEDGEMENTS: (THANK) (YOU)	vi
iii.	PREFACE	xi
iv.	THE *INTRODUCTION*	1

Part One: IN THE BEGINNING

1.	CHAPTER ONE: *PREHIMSTORIC*	11
2.	CHAPTER TWO: *MY STORY*	25

Part Two: THE EVOLUTION

3.	CHAPTER THREE: *"IT'S A SPIRIT!"* - ?	45
4.	CHAPTER FOUR: *HERE'S YOUR DELIVERANCE*	61

Part Three: SETTLED GRACE

5.	CHAPTER FIVE: *LOOSE ENDS*	89
	THE *CONCLUSION*	111

BIBLIOGRAPHY	119
AUTHOR'S BIO	121

PREFACE

My name is Deon Kentell **Williams**,
*(It's been **Thomas** and **Weaver**, before rightfully gaining my birthright),*
And this project is my introduction into authorship.
- It's my first literary baby!

Although new to the published writing scene, I am however, not new to the substance of the subject matter, nor to the gift that makes this possible.

I serve as the Founding Pastor of an Atlanta local ministry in Georgia and have served as such for only over 4-years now upon this 2nd release.

Prior to, and long before now, has been a thorough process over the years, of growing in my relationship with the Lord God primarily, and secondly, in ministry overall, for a sum of about 18 years or so; and counting.

What I'm saying, in other words, is that I come to you **not** as a babe in Christ, but rather, *a man*, who has *put away childish things*!

This work is produced by a mature, meaty, and seasoned relationship with God. - By the Lord's Grace!

I've been often not considered, and hidden from the crowds, and overlooked by certain. I believe it's due to my appearance of not looking the part, *(having a childlike face)* in the minds of some.

- You know, like David; a king, and they didn't even know it.
Nor was he as much as an afterthought, when 'kingship' was up for consideration in his bloodline.
- Like Gideon, who didn't look like a threat, so they let him get close enough to the groves *[in the first place]*, to tear them down. Which was revealed *as such* to me in 2019, when the Lord said that *I am of His secret weapons*. And He said to me, **"how do you think Gideon got close enough to the groves to tear them down?"**
Why, because Gideon was disguised to look like nothing.

In the words of some secular music artist from many years back:
"don't let my cute face fool you!"

- Lastly, Paul the apostle!
We see that he too appeared small in stature but was mighty in the things of God. - *II Cor. 10:10*

My point? Don't miss it, thinking, 'oh that's just Deon!'
I am the LORD's prophet, and this is *my assignment*,
(Of what I hope to be '*of many*' that are to come).

Please note In this material you'll find some instances of what *seems* to be *off* and back *on topic* moments, where I veer from the subject matter slightly to something else. Those moments are what I like to call *Corrective Detouring(s)*. Prerequisites in a sense: Something is being discussed and an opportunity is created to bring to *the Body* **correction** on matters correlated to the Church, that something of the subject matter; *not just the whole theme*, but the topic at the time brought us into in the moment of the text. Relatable to the whole!

DO NOT SKIP

THE INTRODUCTION

INTRODUCTION

Have you taken a look at yourself? Your true self!? I mean, long enough to come to terms with that person!? Maybe you have, while another person reading this hasn't.

This book is dedicated to those who either **have**, **will**, and those who (most frightened by) **refuse** to - **accept,** - the **WHO** of **who they are**.

***

Let me first say, that in the body of this material, that some things at first glance you'll see, may seem contrary to the purpose of this work. But any [valid holding] *"good piece of literature",* has no fear of an *opposing view*! While studying Philosophy *(and Religion)* in college, I learned that you should always welcome the "counterargument". The purpose is, you then locate its flaws and dismantle them! Doing so, helps to build a better case, and further strengthens its' claim!

While on the other hand, not all for the same purpose! Some *contrary seemed* things I'll mention, will be *for no other reason than* to deliver some truths to us church people, who, for some *of us*, I'm sure will find unpopular! Neither perspective has it completely right in the battle between church and the lgbtq. To the Church I say: our understanding has yet to be perfected! We have thought, mistook, and understood certain things differently from what they truly are.

To avoid leaving room for assumption however, ... I tell you plainly, this book's collection of *thought, [Spirit of Truth empowered]* scripture, and lived *experience*, is a work of the Lord, called by God to bring deliverance. And Deliverance in a way, I highly doubt you've heard preached or taught before. Therefore, I must bring clarity, correction, perspective, and truth to the LGBTQ+D Community as well, which is the main objective as to why we're here!

✱✱✱

A Little History

It was 2006 when I first began to understand what's soon to be shared here with you! I don't know when, but at some point, *and as the years passed by*, it became apparent to me, that I was called to share this information! Initially, I imagined I was simply going to preach it in some way, because forming a literature piece was not in my scope of understanding to do so at that time.

By the close of **2016, on *December 14*th,** after coming out of prayer, the Lord spoke to me, saying: *"DO YOU KNOW?"* I said: *"Yeah LORD, I Know."* He said to me: *"IF you know, and you DON'T TELL IT, then by your own profession, you have condemned yourself."*

He told me He was going to hold me accountable! In other words, because I was sure I had encountered Him in that way (which you'll hear about later), it therefore had then become my responsibility, to deliver this to you all along! He desires for others, what He's delivered unto me. Therefore:

To know, and not say, would be my own condemnation.

– SO, I'M SAYING!

HE was speaking to me in such a way, in reference to the fear I had of being shamed and rejected by the church if I said or 'for saying' the things that's now been made available to you in this material! That's why 10 years had passed by, and I still hadn't opened my mouth! [from 2006 – 2016]

As a result of that moment, I said something! *The Lord giving me the date ahead of time*; that on January 1, 2017, I was permitted to share some of the information openly, for the first time via a *Facebook Live* post.

> **To know, and not say, would be my own condemnation.**

Over the years, I became sure I was supposed to tell it, but I didn't know how, and I had no structuring. I became also aware that it was a part of my ultimate, or overall calling!

I mentioned that 10 years had passed by, but it was not time wasted. As to be able to carry such an assignment, I needed time to process it into fruition. The Lord's interest is that to whomever He uses, that they be first partakers of the thing themselves!

(In 2009; three years into, or from the time when I had my divine encounter on this subject, is when I first began to bear the fruit from it, and begin to walk it out, in practice and with application!)

In July of 2019, I had another encounter with the Lord about this matter, and that is when it was made crystal clear to me, that I was to write this book, and that it is *a part of* my prophetic mantle to do so. Not just a calling; but a mantle!

***

Same God

Using scriptural references, let me explain how important I believe this assignment of mine is for someone...

To name a few*: David, Moses;* even *Abraham (according to scripture),* all were prophets of the Lord. Same functionality, but each having individualized assignments! Depending on the assignment, required certain circumstances and preparations!

NOTE for clarity: *The general call or function of* **the prophet,** *is a completely different subject, in which I am* **not** *addressing in this moment nor (at this) time!*

That is why it was of necessity for *"My Story"* and journey to be what it was concerning my desire for men. I can say with confidence in this moment, that it was God who made me what some call a "homosexual", for a greater good, so that I could understand what you will soon know! Those of you shaken by that statement; I submit to you, that God is far bigger than you know, and is calculated beyond our most complicated equation. The Lord loves them, and more than we give Him credit for!

Here's an example!
The same way the Lord devised a plan (Christ) to save ALL mankind from the *"Fall" / consequences* of Adam's sin; consider this! – Is it too farfetched to consider, that this Same God, Whose desire, is that not one soul be lost *(John 6:39, II Peter 3:9),* to believe that He would raise up men and women of the Lord who

were given a same sex attraction, with the intent to deliver them, and *(like Moses)* send them Back into that sphere *(Like Egypt)* to bring out the others? – *c.f. (The Book of Exodus)*

***

All Aboard!

So, buckle your seatbelts and get ready for this ride! I forewarn you however, once you have taken this in, I tell you ahead of time, that it means that God is now calling you **UP** to that place. For the Lord refuses to whoop us with many stripes according to the Bible, concerning that which **we do not know**.

However, once you **know it**, you are expected to live by it.

Luke 12:47-48 King James Version (KJV)

47 And that servant, <u>which</u> <u>knew</u> his lord's will, and prepared not himself, neither did according to his will, shall be beaten with <u>many</u> <u>stripes</u>.
48 But he that <u>knew</u> <u>not</u>, and did commit things worthy of stripes, shall be beaten with <u>few</u> <u>stripes</u>. For unto whomsoever much is given, of him shall be much required: and to whom men have committed much, of him they will ask the more.

There it is! – Because once you know, you gain responsibility of your knowledge increased.

Also, Jesus says in *St John 8:32 (KJV)*:

"And ye shall know the truth, and the truth shall make you free"

It is often said: "the truth shall make you free". Not So!

The revelation of this is as such: The truth is the truth, whether you are aware of it or not. The proper interpretation of this passage is that it is the KNOWING / knowledge of truth that frees you; not just truth itself! You must first become aware of truth before you can apply it!

To my same-gender-loving brothers and sisters out there, herein is your clarion call, with *"what do I do about serving God fully, but I know my desire is for the same sex!?"* Don't get ahead of me! None of what you will find on the following pages will be remotely close to the preaching you've commonly heard preached in some churches, which often places this one thing on a pedestal (of sin) and overlooks everything else.

I submit a truth to you, because I have walked through it, and I have been anointed to help you understand this: *"How do I deal with both?"* Your answers are only a few pages away, but promise me, you'll take the full ride.

No one gets on a roller coaster, and in the middle of the loop, jumps off *(ultimately, killing themselves)*, because they changed their mind midway. They bare the ride, hoping that it's over soon, at best. So once this train pulls off from the station, stay with me until we're at the next stop ahead: "Deliverance!"

Now without further or due. The reason I began this work with the question posed, is because it will be vital that you be honest with yourself about *you*.

In other words, in order that you get the fullness of this powerful teaching, it is a must that you come out of hiding. – Not necessarily with others, but with yourself. If you, (for example) are a man, who engages in ANY (same) sexual practices, or maybe they're not practices in deeds; maybe the desire for it is just there and *you haven't acted on it*. Well, you have got to be honest with yourself and accept that there is some part of you / who you are, that is gay!

Someone may say, "I'm not gay, I don't care what you say!" – "I've never actually done it."

Well, my friend, Jesus the Christ is recorded saying in:

St. Matthew 5:27, 28 (KJV)
27 Ye have heard that it was said by them of old time, Thou shalt not commit adultery:
28 But I say unto you, That whosoever looketh on a woman to lust after her hath committed adultery with her already in his heart.

Therefore, whether you've acted on it or not, or whether you've permitted yourself to only go but so far, etc. Or whatever your mental cushion may be that's used to convince yourself that you don't fall into the "gay" or lesbian category, Jesus is telling you, that if the thoughts or desires are even there; *yoouuu'rrreee guilty!* And my point for saying this is none other than for the following!

God can't help you if you're still lying to yourself. God honors honesty. He can help us when we get honest with ourselves, and with HIM.

I'm excited! – So, let's get started.

Side note:
And that is what prayer is, Having honest talks with the Lord. Maybe that is why some things are not answered for us, because we're not honest!

We sometimes get so accustomed to wearing mask for the world, that we forget to take them off when we go before The Lord to pray. And He sees behind them, but because you're not honest, He can't help you! Because, although the Lord sees who we really are; consider this!

James 4:2 says: *"We have not, because **we** ask not"*
And something's won't ever get answered, until **"we"** show up; not *(the mask of)* who we pretend to be.

Part One: ***IN THE BEGINNING***

CHAPTER 1:
PREHIMSTORIC

CHAPTER 1:

PREHIMSTORIC

THE PREREQUISITE

My name is Deon; and I was born on a Sabbath; *Saturday, October 25, 1980, in Atlanta, GA, U.S.A.*

    I say this, to introduce myself and so you can perhaps grab a better visual of the pictures painted for you here in this and following chapter(s). For instance: If I say something along the lines of: *"It was 1992"*, then you know that I was between the ages of 11 or 12, depending upon if that date in *"1992"* was before or after the 25th of October.

    Furthermore, this section, *nor book* is about my *"Life Story"/ Autobiography*. But pertains only to the story of my Life regarding my sexual orientation(s), identity, and the evolution of the man whom you now have before you, with the hope of only a positive impact on the lives of all those who choose to read that which is written within.

PRESTORY

When I Think of Home

I was raised in a Christian home, by my mom and maternal grandparents! Although we lived separately outside of the home of my grandparents; (the Late *Elder Willis Walker Weaver, Jr.*, and the Late *Elder Ruby [Horton] Weaver*), we spent so much time with them and in their home, that my sister, *Cheywana* and I, were literally still raised by our grandparents, in addition to that of our mother's rearing.

The love of my grandparents was astounding. Now, here you have two ordained Elders in the Christian Faith, who had *four* sons, and *one* daughter; (*my mother Shirley; a minister of the Gospel as well.*)

(*Now excuse me for going off on a tangent here concerning the following, but it is a prerequisite to a point that I am now in the process of making!*)

Of those *four* sons, *one* of them were gay; the Late *Nathaniel Weaver*; the youngest of their *five* children. I'm mentioning this for a reason; stay with me!

After discovering that their son was *same gender loving*, they never exiled him. Not once had I ever heard them talk about him negatively and his choices in his absence. They genuinely loved their son. And although (the fact is) they were (not only) Bible believers but were preachers of this Bible as well; they accepted him! I can recall *Nay,* as we affectionately called him, invited his boyfriend over for holiday dinners, and no one mistreated them or acted funny as I can recall, *(still being a child at the time myself)*. Regardless of what someone could negatively gather about my grandparent's actions here, they did what we are all ultimately commanded to do, which is to **love.** You don't know what their prayer life was like, or if they stayed on their faces for "deliverance" for their child - (*the outside, looking in,* church folk version of *deliverance,* that is!)

But even after we come out of prayer, and whatever our position is, and whatever the Bible says, and after we've declared His word, it is never given by example in the Bible, that **position** becomes a legitimate authority over *(or an excuse for the lack of)* the act of **Love**! You do not have to agree with someone's choices; no! You can even take a stand for holiness; etc., but that is NEVER an excuse not to love. God hates sin. Not the sinner!

Anybody that knows the Word of God, knows the authority of the Word of the Lord. Such as in **ISAIAH 55:11**, where the Lord speaks through His prophet, that His Word will not return to Him void, but that it shall stand, and accomplish what it was sent to do. We also know that in **MATTHEW 24:35**, Jesus, *the Christ* Himself says:

"*Heaven and earth shall pass away, but my words shall not pass away.*"

But this is why **Ephesians 4:15** bridges the gap between the *WHO of Who God Is*, and the interconnectivity (and Authority) of His Word. It says that we are to speak the ***truth – in Love***. It is an expression and understanding of the duality of "God" at its best! Yes preachers, the Word doesn't change, and we must stand on it, and even the Lord Himself is unmovable in What He has established (and says), but He Never stops being *WHO* He is in the process.

1 John 4:7-10 King James Version (KJV)
7 Beloved, let us love one another: for love is of God; and every one that loveth is born of God, and knoweth God.
*8 He that loveth not, knoweth not God; **for God is love**.*
9 In this was manifested the love of God toward us, because that God sent his only begotten Son into the world, that we might live through him.
10 Herein is love, not that we loved God, but that he loved us, and sent his Son to be the propitiation for our sins.

In other words, because **God IS Love**, He never stops being Himself, just to enact a **position**. For God is both *Good* (Love) and *Just*. It is unfortunately people, who do not know how to be both. It is a large percentage of church people, who tend to sometimes be low on the ability to keep God's word, stand on it, don't live in compromise, not be hypocritical; yet STILL, ultimately not move from "Love" as it relates to dealing with those who have yet to come to where they are!

Concerning *v.10,* what's to be understood is this: If God didn't love us while we were not yet WHO we were to become, then there would have been no hope for us *(The recipients of Salvation)* either. If He reached us through love, why is He not to do the same for the lost/not yet Saved!?

> *"For God so loved the world, that he gave his only begotten Son, that whosoever believeth in him should not perish, but have everlasting life."* **– St. John 3:16 (KJV)**

***

Evil and Good (detour)

When I say that God is both **good and just,** let me break that down. Being a seminarian student, I've heard others argue that God is good and evil, speaking of the "bad" things that happen to people, and in this world. Referencing how bad things happen to "good" people; (*although the Messiah, in Mark 10:18 says that there is absolutely, not anyone that's good but the Father in Heaven).* And how *'good people'* die or die young, thus, *they say,* so God must be evil as well as good! That's completely foolish!

There is no evil in the Lord God. The Lord is "good", *merciful* and kind. Patient, and everything else!

As a matter of fact, or you ready for a hard truth to hear? The Lord is so merciful, that in His sovereignty and ability to see *and knowing of all*, He may sometime take, or allow a person's life to be taken away from here early, rather than give them long life because in some cases, taking them away 'early', or at the time He takes them, is a preservative of their souls being saved *then*, versus letting them live on, if their 'lived' future would result in an eternity not inclusive of Him! Because the biblical requirement is to endure until the end, *(Matthew 24:13)* and if we can't hold on to what the end should be, sometimes the end is shortened to preserve the soul altogether! [Think of Matthew 24:22; Mark 13:20]

Consider this also, why the supposed *good people* die as such!

Isaiah 57:1 (KJV)
The righteous perisheth, and no man layeth it to heart:
and merciful men are taken away, none considering that
the righteous is taken away from the evil to come.

The NLT [New Living Translation] literally says, "good people"!

In other case's However, there are spiritual (and natural) laws of **sowing and reaping.**

Some things happen simply, as a result of the Lord's **justice system.** Something that we falsely accuse "God" of being evil for, is Him being 'Just' instead. After all, "vengeance belongs to the Lord." – **Deuteronomy 32:35.** That doesn't make Him any part evil. He doesn't even have to do anything! The spiritual law is already in motion, from the beginning. I guess you'd have to have the definition so that it truly makes sense!

JUST =
1. Based on or behaving according to what is morally right and fair.

2. (of treatment) deserved or ***appropriate in the circumstance****(s).*

Now think of the natural law of *sowing & reaping's* of harvests.

It means fairness, a balancing in some sorts.

The Lord is quick to forgive us when we truly repent of our sin with a sincere heart. In the Introduction, *Luke 12:47, 48* is included concerning there being a difference in punishment, which is more severe for those of us who already knew better and chose to engage in sin anyway. So, although the Lord will immediately forgive those who sincerely repent of our sin, but in some cases, His forgiveness does not free us from still reaping a harvest of whatever seed we've planted. Even still, when you've truly repented, even if there are some things you must reap; it is seasoned with so much grace, that it is not as harsh as what it should truly be.

So sometimes, *(and using 'the above' as only one example of what I'm trying to explain)*, God's automatic *sowing and reaping* **justice system**, is 'evil' spoken of, and ignorantly, we declare and accuse *the Lord our God* of being evil, as well; good. There's no such thing! To be both would show partiality in the totality of God, which would make the Lord not perfect. Our god is only Love.

His word tells us not to be *partial, compromised, double minded*, nor *lukewarm*. Having *singleness of eye*; *choosing the Lord's side*: not able to *serve two masters*, but we dare say that what the Lord requests and requires of us, that He's not that Himself!?

Some people sound deep, but in actuality; are foolish. And lastly, if you don't have a true solid foundation in God; in relationship with Him for real, I recommend, not going to seminary!

> MATTHEW 12:25; MARK 3:25 KJV
> 25 And Jesus knew their thoughts, and said unto them, Every kingdom divided against itself is brought to desolation; and every city or house divided against itself shall not stand:
> 25 And if a house be divided against itself, that house cannot stand.

(End detour)

***

The Polar Opposite

It was what I heard in the church from preachers behind the bookboard in the pulpit that shaped a different / (what I thought to be) / full understanding of homosexuality. It was partially right, but not completely.

In the 80's and 90's as a child, it was a common thing somewhere in the church at large, at any given time, to hear a preacher say "it's an abomination", and in most cases, it was accompanied by some insulting term of *punk, faggot, or sissy* hurled into the congregation, not caring who it hit while they were up preaching the Lord's Word (And some still do it!) – Might I add, I had not yet come to "My Story" of when I began to develop a desire for a man, when initially hearing these things.

And it was the preacher saying it, so it had to be right; *right*!? It was believable. I took it as all facts! BUT before we deal with what's wrong, let's be clear to accept the portions that are scripturally sound, right, or correct; thus: for clarity's sake, before we proceed, ...

The Bible does say in **Leviticus 18:22** - *"Thou shalt not lie with mankind, as with womankind: it is abomination."*

What this text means, is that two men should NOT have sex with one another. And I'm not here to debate that. However, the same preachers who love to hurl "it's an abomination", for some reason seem to use their ALL-MIGHTY Executive power to change the Word of God, to dismiss ALL of the other "Abominations" they fall prey to listed in the Bible; (most of them within the same chapter or book). Isn't that peculiar! Yes, I'm calling hypocrisy to the carpet, while on my way to helping my LGBTQD*ownlow* brothers and sisters in Christ.

I'm even realizing, as this body of work is taking shape, that it is not solely to bring the LGBTQ Christian into Full truth of their same sex desire, but that it is to bring understanding to other Christians on the outside looking in, thinking that they have the formula. It is to debunk *(due to lack of understanding)*, their version of Deliverance from the homosexual **practicing** Lifestyle.

With *1 John 4:7-10* in mind, from the *'Prestory'* section, let's go deeper. Here's the connection!

Therefore, if love (God) is in you, then why should it be so difficult to tell someone what the Lord says His **position** is, on whatever subject matter, without feeling the need or deeming it necessary, to utilize vulgar and derogatory remarks, mingled in with **truth**, that, guess what; *stands*, *speaks,* and *speaks up* for Itself?

In other words, if Love is in me, I ought to be able to plainly tell someone who's a Fornicator = *(someone who's having sex outside of marriage)* that God says: what you are doing is called "fornication", and that it is sin, and sin separates you from Him, without calling him or her out of their name in the process. It's usually done, in an intended to offend type of way I believe!

Verse 8 of **1 John 4** above says, if it's not love, God isn't in you! We must ALL, as ministers of the gospel *(to whom this applies)*, check our motives, and understanding of why we're preaching. Is it because you want to be right so bad? Is it that you're just happy you found one thing you can get right, so you shame the ones who haven't!? Or is it because YOU are genuinely concerned about a soul other than your own?

If I am God and I AM Love, and I say you can't *(let's say for example)* have sex with someone that you're not married to, without it being unacceptable to *Me*; {which is the classification of what *I* call (**sin**: *that which is contrary to what I say)*} then that is *My* **position** on the matter. It is (the "Word of God" because *I* (the Lord God have spoken and decided on it). However, in *My* "position", *I* cannot separate myself from Who and What *I Am*; "Love". Therefore, *I* mean what *I* say, but *I* speak with intentionality because it is *I, Love*, Who produced this decision for your well-being. Which is *My* position, produced by Love. – So church, where is ours?

What are our motives?

The LORD says His positions are what they are because they are housed and formulated from Him; "Love".

*I tell you - you cannot do these things (MY position), because **I** - **AM** – **Love**(s) you, and **I AM** trying to keep you from the harm you will bring to yourself, through what sin produces.*

Where is our Love?

We clearly state our positions to people as we preach to them, but what are our motives! God's stance and motives is out of Love. So, again I say, church, where is ours? And what are our motives if it isn't love? Why do you preach the truth, if not driven by Love?

Many preachers are preaching and operating from "hate" rather than Love. I've watched some of them. There seems to be a strong disdain and hatred when homosexuality comes up. Many people, not just leaders, find themselves on the pedestal of *better than* in those moments, placing same sex "sin" on a "pedestal of sin". But if I be a Bible reader and practitioner, I recall the scripture saying there is not one sin category unforgiveable *(greater)* than any other, other than blasphemy of the Holy Ghost. – *St. Matthew 12:31*

Proverbs 6:16-19 King James Version (KJV)

*16 These six things doth the Lord hate: yea, seven are an **abomination** unto him:*

17 A proud look, a lying tongue, and hands that shed innocent blood,

18 An heart that deviseth wicked imaginations, feet that be swift in running to mischief,

19 A false witness that speaketh lies, and he that soweth discord among brethren.

THIS MUST BE DOCUMENTED

Oh, you dodged those, Great! But do you eat Catfish? Squid? Any Shellfish such as: Shrimp? Scallop? Crab? Lobster? - Just to name a few!

> **Leviticus 11:9-12 King James Version (KJV)**
> *⁹ These shall ye eat of all that are in the waters: whatsoever hath fins and scales in the waters, in the seas, and in the rivers, them shall ye eat.*
> *¹⁰ And all that have not fins and scales in the seas, and in the rivers, of all that move in the waters, and of any living thing which is in the waters, they shall be an **abomination** unto you:*
> *¹¹ They shall be even an **abomination** unto you; ye shall not eat of their flesh, but ye shall have their carcases in **abomination**.*
> *¹² Whatsoever hath no fins nor scales in the waters, that shall be an **abomination** unto you.*

Yep. Most of us are abominable in The Lord's sight. (But for the record, I don't eat that stuff!) So why are those doing "abominable" things in one category, not outcast, while out-casting others, doing "abominable" things in another?

***

So, to recap, I grew up in a family of preachers, and in a home, where I was taught how to love a person, even if I am to hate the sin, <u>Vs</u>. hearing other preachers insult gay folk and preach almost as if it were from hatred, when trying to convey that homosexuality is wrong.

***

Now on with *my* actual *story*, but there's just one last thing!

My righteous brothers and sisters who are living for God, please don't be easily offended. If Apostle Paul could write to you and tell you he was once a murderer, and you still read and preach (from) him, then you can bare me being honest with my past.

And as it pertains to detail. This book wasn't made for the - what we've decided would be the "church norm", nor for the church norm's approval or opinion. It is specifically, or mainly for the gay and lesbian individual to be introduced to real deliverance; (one that you, who Are offended, have not been able to offer them.) Thus, I choose to be transparent and honest about my Life pertaining to how I became a practicing "homosexual" in my past. Why? Because, my LGBTQ friends must *first* know that I understand them, and that I'm not speaking from an outside perspective, before they can believe the validity of what I have to say on the Flip!

CHAPTER 2:
MY STORY

CHAPTER 2:

MY STORY

THE STORY TOLD

Note: All names have been altered to maintain Anonymity.

It was at the age of 15! *I never once thought about this until a few moments ago, that my desire for a man became apparent to me, synonymously to the point of puberty: sometime after.* Prior to this age, I had girlfriends beforehand, and since then! The last one; at the age of 19. This one devised a plan; deciding to lie to me about being pregnant. False 'positive' results from the "doctor" and all, included!

Upon discovery, was the tipping point from remaining bi-sexual, *[which she was aware of]*, to being completely turned off from women in that type of way at the time. Despite her knowledge *of*, and her liking *for* ladies as well, I chose not to engage nor entertain any men, so long as I was with her. But after the pregnancy scam and ending the relationship, I became completely / solely interested in men!

Regressing,

I had technically had sex for the first time at age 10 while the other participant was 9. She initiated it and was very advanced. I think someone of the adult male species had introduced her, if you catch my drift; we'll say it that way! I am not for sure, but she knew A lot to be 9. At ten I don't think I could get an erection just yet. I can't remember, but I put it in! Well anyway, she and I did this on the regular, being that, while my mom was going to cosmetology school in the afternoon, her mother and stepfather kept me from the time I got out of school until my mother came home. They were our neighbors on *Bolton Rd* where I grew up. Our apartments didn't have a sign for its name displayed outside, so I never knew it, but it sits directly across from the apartment complex that was once named *Esquire Village* at the time; *the name's since been changed!*

This was not my only sexual encounter with a female. I've had a few since, after puberty. It was those few encounters I can undoubtably say, we had sex!

Back to age 15 however! Having had a sexual encounter or two with the opposite sex by then, and having had some girlfriends, I knew I was 'straight'. But one day out of the blue; *(by then, we had moved from Atlanta to College Park / from College Park to Union City)*, something happened and challenged all of that!

In 1995; Living in Union City, I was sitting outside in the breezeway of our building, on the stair rail, when a guy walked by, and in my mind, I heard myself say something to the effect of "he's cute".

[*see pictured*] – *Captured Feb. 7, 2020; [25yrs later].*

To your Left, is the Actual Building and View that I saw looking out into the parking lot.

To your Right, as if you were looking from the lot towards the bldg. where I sat.

One Major difference is, I don't recall those iron rails. I recall that the rails at the time were wooden, I believed them to be! I'm almost certain.

 &

Left pic. {Looking out, I was sitting on Rail to your LEFT.}

Right pic. {Looking toward bldg., I was sitting to your RIGHT.}

Now the *funny* / (what might not seem to make sense) *part* about it is this. The person that I had my very first "gay" thought for, was someone that I had seen regularly. We lived in the same apartment complex and rode the same school bus at one point. He was two grades higher than me, so when I was in the sixth, he was in the eighth grade, and we rode the same bus only then, but by then when I had the liking of him, he was in high school, and I was in middle school but in eight grade myself by now.

So, to my surprise, someone I had seen on many days prior to this day, was the recipient to my very first moment of gay consciousness. Because prior to any other time seeing him, (or any other guy for that matter), there was nothing. Not an inkling, and not a clue! Nothing in another man moved me prior to that day. But once "that day" happened, I couldn't, (and in a sense, still haven't been able to) shake it. – *That part will make sense after a while.*

Immediately I started going crazy on myself within my thoughts. Excuse me for just a moment, but this is what I said *within*, and I remember this vividly; "*oh hell nawl, I know I ain't gay*", with a series of other thoughts following, beating myself up and telling myself (outwardly at this point) "*you trippin*"; etc.

For days, even months, there was a battle going on within, from the moment that I ever - out of the clear blue, recognized there was something about a man that I liked! Months flew by, until one day I finally gave in. And my thoughts went from fighting and refusing, to now: "*I wonder*", "*what would it be like to be with another dude*". Again, this was months later after that dreadful day!

Then after "I wonder" finally transpired, another series of months passed by, just entertaining the thought. It wasn't until those few months took its course and I finally gave up on hoping, and (then) saying to myself: "*it's not going to ever happen*", "*There's no one else out there like that*", that ironically someone else from my same neighborhood suddenly started coming around me and knocking on my door.

✳✳✳

– And then there was *Payton*. –

Just like that other guy whose name is *"O.C."* that I had that first male attraction to, I saw *Payton* on a regular basis as well. Even more so than O.C., because Payton did not only live in my neighborhood, but for sure rode the same school bus daily with me. But he and I never talked or hung out! But one day out of the blue; very shortly after going from "I wonder" to finally arriving at "it's not going to happen" months later, Payton knocked on my door one day. That was the day we started hanging and talking to each other.

Not long after, he suggested one of us spend the night at the others house. I can specifically remember him wanting to spend the night at my house. We both worked up the nerves to ask our mother's. My mother agreed, but his mother said no. So, we not long afterwards gave it another shot! We asked this time if I could spend the night there, and Payton's mother said *yes,* this time.

So here we are that night. (His sister had a crush on me by the way). So much so, that she slept on the floor in his room that night, instead of in her bed in her own bedroom. Maybe it had something to do with their male cousin *Mikey* being over that night as well. All four of us were slumbering in Payton's room, but Payton and I had the bed.

Well, during the day, and prior to nightfall, it was just the two of us, kicking it in his bedroom. At the time, Super Nintendo was extremely popular and the most recent and hottest gaming system out. We both owned one, but I had *Super Street Fighter II: Turbo* and brought it over to his house to play, (although *Zelda* was and is probably still my most favorite of all time!) But while playing the game, we had somehow made a bet!

As we're playing Street Fighter, he blurts out: *"let's make a bet!"*. I asked what kind, and he said so. To not be too graphic, it pertained to that of the oral kind. Who won determined who did what! So, after agreeing, I began to put a good spanking on him on the game. Maybe I got excited, but that's what happened! Time is passing after that moment, and I'm thinking about it throughout the day; especially after winning. I pondered and pondered, until (although it took a long time to do), I worked up the nerve to bring it up, and say *"so what's up with that bet?"* I assumed he would say something like: "hell nawl man, you gay as hell" and we'd laugh it off, joking and "joning" each other like teenage boys do: But that's not what happened! What did happen was him saying: *"I don't know"* instead. Immediately, my thoughts went into overdrive, thinking to myself, *("oh he was really serious. Otherwise, 'I don't know' wouldn't've even been an option!")*

So later we're in bed, and things start to happen. While sister and Cousin Mikey are in the room sleep by now. We eased our way out of the room, and into the bathroom, where nearly everything went down. If there were someone watching, it would've taken a lot of convincing them that it was both our first times, because everything flowed so "naturally". We heard one of the adult's footsteps/movement in the house, from them getting up and going to their bathroom in the back, and it spooked us.

Well, we first moved into the sister's room, come to think of it, but after hearing the movement, we then moved from there to the hallway bathroom. For it was more likely for an adult to walk into a bedroom to check on their little girl*('s room)*, than to walk in on someone "using" the bathroom! - But the bathroom is where the most activity took place!

After that night, Payton and I no longer needed to spend the night to create that space. We now know what's up. And he'd come over during the day. As I think back, I don't know how we got away with that in my mom and stepdad's apartment.

Payton had a distinct scent, and I could smell his scent in my nostril without him even being around. But it would only happen when he was on the way to visit. By the way, there were no phone calls and heads-ups. I would smell his scent and five minutes later, there he was, knocking on the door. Payton kept this up for a few months. I'm still 15 at the time; he was 14! Fooling with him, we ended up having sex with a girl from the neighborhood named *Mandy* that we would get with as a joint venture; I remember it being at least twice! I'm trying to keep my words as simmered as I can while sharing this story. I thought it was such a turn-on, having her collectively, knowing our own little secret.

I didn't have another sexual encounter with another male until I was close to sixteen, when I got to high school in the Fall of '96.

I must have had to be freshly turned 15 when I had that first "he's cute" thought sitting outside that day concerning O.C., because remember, that happened and then the immediate fighting and denial within myself occurred. Then months passed and I gave in (to just the thought). Then more months passed by, and I got to the point of believing no one else was out there to bring the curiosity to reality. Then a little time passed and then it happened, and it lasted for months. But even then, it was a long period of time before I had another sexual encounter with another guy, but I do remember it being a good while passing from the time of Payton and I's escapade to that of having another encounter with another male, (which again, happened sometime after entering 9th grade.)

What we had lasted a while, until my wallet went missing, and I accused him of stealing it, and *Leon* (a newly appointed friend once entering high school) and I, called ourselves "outing" him to some of our peers in Payton and I's apartment complex. Only to later discover that the wallet was lodged in a jacket pocket in my closet. I felt (and still to this day, feel) so bad about falsely accusing him, and allowing my new friend to help influence me to think that telling his business was cool. That was messy as heck. (I was 15 y'all; and influenced, forgive me! – It was my friend's idea). I don't know if I ever got a chance to apologize to him, he moved away shortly afterwards. Not his family; just him. He went to stay with his dad I believe. Years and years later, into my adulthood, I discovered from another old neighborhood friend I happened to have run into around Atlanta, at *Five Points Transit Station*, that Payton had passed away from a Brain Aneurysm. I was so hurt to hear that.

***

Boyhood

I would live out my teen years trying to be grown.

On *October 31, 1996*, six days after my 16th birthday, a high-school friend, who happened to be my first boyfriend, who, in which introduced me to the concept of boyfriends, (yep, *Leon*), invited me over to his place to skip school that day.

Before I go forward; two things you must know:

One; prior to meeting Leon, my gay brain hadn't developed that far into even considering or knowing that two guys could "go together". I just thought it was some sexual curiosity thing!

Secondly; during the date at-hand, we were no longer boyfriends. We were boyfriends for a very short time until I went to him and said: *"I don't think we are supposed to be together in a relationship: I think we are supposed to be friends"*. To my surprise, he easily accepted. There was no backlash, and we instantly shifted into friendship without a single beat skipped. What I "felt" turned out to be accurate because we became "best friends" for over two decades, and from there, I was privileged to become his pastor in later years! Well, by the time that this date mentioned above came about, we were good and locked into our friendship.

So here we are, on Halloween '96. I called another friend *Akeem* who was a little older and had access to his mother's car and told him of the invitation. He came and picked me up, and we were on our way to Leon's house! Six of us skipped school that day, plus Akeem, who was 19 years old and graduated already at the time, and a Seven-man-brotherhood was instantaneously formed that day! This friendship became more precious to me than I could ever explain. We went and grabbed pizza that day. All 7 of us piled up in Akeem's mother's Purple Nissan Altima, and he treated us to *Pizza Hut*. We were inseparable from that day forth!

Each year we came together for what we called our Anniversary. I'm laughing thinking about this, but I'll share a poem I wrote for us, during our 18th year Friendship Anniversary, simply entitled **Friends**.

> In 1996 on this date mis amores. A Thursday, early morning, time for school, what a bore!
> Little did I know, this day, everything will change, God had a plan that a meeting would be arranged.
> Got a call from my friend, that he was skipping school, well this was rather strange, before this Moment, I Thought this kid, he followed all the rules.
> Whether He was feeling spicy or what, he never said, I don't Know. He said some guys were coming over, and he wanted me to show. Hmm!
> So, I picked up the phone and called my dearest-dearest friend, I

told him what was going on, With Excitement, convinced him, "let us attend!"

What if he had said no? What if I had gone to school?

What If every moment on every hand; one alteration, And the bond could've never been glued!?

The purple car arose, to the occasion, yes it did. *Virginia Ave. here we come, we bout to go pop the Kids!*

Ha ha ha, I'm just kidding, we never talked like that, we was the Trade, Atlanta boiz, and I'll just Leave it at that!

So anywho, we arrive, (Leon) opens the door.

We go in, just a couple were there; we're waiting on (David) And (Pisario).

How could I forget that day, I walked outside to meet those two, with our host, Observing them from afar. Walking down the street, they bopped, their way into our hearts.

Now we're all Here, and (Akeem) puts on a show, feeling fab and feeling grand, I knew him, but nobody liked that Whore.

They Thought that he was bougie, but he just feeling -he- meant no hurt. They found out pretty quickly, he was the coolest guy on Earth!

He even bought us pizza, he piled us in his car, the Seven dwarfs: it was I, (Patrick), (Akeem), (Leon), (Ryan), (David), and (Pisario)!

Rest In Peace to our friend, we miss Him, for all of us, this Is For sure.

(Patrick) connected us to (Ben). And (Albert), we're glad you showed.

You guys are the best friends Ever.

18 years and going strong, soldiers, Because God has made us so.

Oct. 31, 2014
Author and friend,

These are the group of friends that I would spend my teenage and young adult years, "trying to be grown" with, as I mentioned earlier. That special day in '96 occurred on a Thursday and the last day of October. – So, not the immediate weekend as in two days later, but the weekend following, these same group of newly appointed friends shared our 2nd memory together of many others to come. We were taken to a gay club for the very first time, by our slightly older friend Akeem, – A whole new world to get lost in, and to get plenty of practice with the *trying to be grown* thing again.

***

Party Hardy

Being underage, we were snuck through the downstairs backdoor of this club. Not long after this night, we all went to get fake I.D.'s, but still found ourselves downstairs "backdooring it" on the regular most times; I guess because even with fake I.D.'s, someone letting us in through this way, still meant free entry. And yes, I did say regularly. We were at the club almost every other weekend, at 15*(Leon)*; the rest of us, 16 and 17 years old, with 19-year-old Akeem.

    I can only be in one place at one time, thus, I don't know what my friends experienced personally after we were exposed to all that comes with what is called *'the gay'* or *'club'* "scene", but when I think about a few experiences of mine, I can easily say looking back, that my age was tried to be taken advantage of slightly; nothing horrific however! I think the thing that probably protected me from being victimized by some situations *that I never knew about*, (because The Lord blocked them of course), were probably due to my being upstanding in this regard and being brought up on godly integrity. I can remember some older guys trying to get with me, and someone would say, *"you better talk to him; he got…"* They'd insert the word *money*, or this type of *car*, or whatever there was that the person saying it *at the time* seemed to be impressed by.

My Story

But I remember several times telling those people that I'm not going to talk to somebody just because of what they have if my interest isn't in the person themselves! As an adult, I see how it could be easy *to think* that you can attract a youngster with that type of stuff, but I was not one of those youngsters, and I think it saved me from some situations!

I remember Leon, Patrick, and I, were taken to North Carolina with some slightly older guys than ourselves, which took us lightly shopping; like a pair of Old Navy swimming trunks or something. I didn't realize it at the time, but it came to me years later out of the clear blue while reminiscing. - They were up there boosting, i.e., *writing bad checks.* The guys were! The guy who was interested in me thought I was going to have sex with him, because he bought me a few $12 to $15 Old Navy items. No, it's not that the price mattered either. The point is, I wasn't going to be bought or coerced to do anything I wasn't doing of my own decision making and free-will. Wow, God gave me some good sense back then. I've made more foolish decision after coming into adulthood, than as a teenager exposed to things where I could've made some really foolish choices!

And of course, there were some guys I actually did like and did have moments with. I wasn't an angel. And I certainly was Not then, what I was to now become. So yes, I did explore my sexuality! Remember, I gave up the idea of ever having this happen due to thinking no other man was "like that". It took forever for Payton to manifest, then a while for Leon to do so as well: *(Leon's the person I had my next encounter with (besides Payton), during that short space of time he and I were boyfriends, before we quickly shifted to letting that go, and becoming friends).*

With that said, so to think that a man who likes another man was scarce, which was my reality, to the discovery that there is a whole other world out there where there is a plethora of men who feel the same way as you: no guessing games involved, and based on *"the scene"*, you don't have to wonder if they're gay or not! - So yes, I had my share of experiences!

But let's focus for a moment, about me trying to be grown. Although we skipped school that one day when our brotherly friendship began, but after being introduced to "the scene", some of us: (I know Leon and I for sure), begin to skip school regularly. So much so, that at age 18, I took the route of an alternative school where I received my GED. Not because I wasn't smart enough to get through high school, but because I had gotten so far behind from being out of school more than being there, that I chose that option as an easier way out, rather than just simply catching up. Young minds are so funny! I couldn't dare just buckle down and catch up on a little work for the time I had wasted; and cut into my fun / "trying to be grown" times; oh no! I was being lazy about what was important. We live and learn, right!

I remember hearing one of my former pastors once say: "sin will always take you further than you intended to go." If that isn't true!

***

Party of a Different Kind
I spent most of my youth (age 19-25) in a relationship with a man *(Edward)* who didn't know how to love me. Although he did love me; I can't take that from him, but it was very dysfunctional! I lost myself completely over the course of the years. It wasn't even his fault.

For a season, (believe it or not), I was his assignment! So, I was sheltered from all that came with *(being with)* him, until one day I heard the Lord tell me it was time to let it go. That my assignment (for him) was done! I disobeyed and stayed in the relationship beyond the point of grace. It was then, and only then, that I started to lose myself. – *DISOBEDIENCE is* Very Dangerous.

At the time, I had always smoked weed from *like* age 16 and up, but at the point of the beginning of this relationship, it was 1999 when we met, and 2000 when it was made official. Years after that; maybe 2005, my defenses were down, and I had really begun to lose myself. But even in 2001, (during one of our relationships off seasons), was the first time I popped an ecstasy pill. That was something I thought I'd never do: a drug of any sort other than the natural herb of marijuana! –

[And NO, I'm not saying it that way to condone Disciples of Christ smoking weed. I am Not. – The Body is the temple of the Holy Ghost!] – *I Corinthians 6:19-20*

But *Edward* and I's *on and off again* relationship persisted; (far after God said let it go), which was probably around 2003, and my defenses were still getting weaker. By then, we were popping X like skittles with each other. 2005 was the last time we tried being together, when he came to live with me in my Loft Apt in the city. Although the relationship was finally over, after five long years of this *up* and *down* drama with him; I was zapped! - Giving so much of myself to what I considered to be at the time 'the love of my Life'!

- But it takes time for things to manifests outwardly once we've opened the door to certain spirits inwardly.

By 2007, I found myself hitting the crackpipe for the first time. I kept it under wraps from my peoples; friends and all, but I was out there. Not stealing and wilding out, but out there as in, it had a hold on me. My hustle would be to post up at the gas station and tell people I was out of gas. And truth be told, the gas light stayed on, so actually / technically I wasn't lying! So, whatever I got, I'd put probably $2 in the tank, and the rest, was my crack money.

It didn't last but a few months; That addiction, as bad as it had me. After the first hit, I went on a 3-month binge, but then stopped cold turkey. Then months passed by, then I'd go out again. One day, after being in and out like that, and my family finding out, my mother invited me to come to a "Deliverance Service" at her *then* church home, *Paradise COGIC*. It was one night during the week; a Thursday I believe! I went to the altar and cried out. It wasn't even the high that I was tired of. It was all the crap *(dealing with others in their addictions)* that came with it, that was too much to deal with! But either way, I was tired of being bound.

I cried out and the Lord took it instantly. I even tried to go back once months later after that, and the Lord said to me, He allowed it so I could see, that the spirit which was behind it, was gone. It was a feeling of pointlessness. I didn't feel anything.

But in **2008** it happened again.

I wrote a poem entitled: *What Happened?* during this second bout with Crack Cocaine. And the Lord delivered again after I wrote this letter on my computer to Him out of the depths of my soul!

"WHAT HAPPENED?"

What happened to the standards instilled into me as a child?
What happened to the purity that drew so many with my smile?
What happened to the days I'd be minding my own business and YOU would stop me; instructing me to pray?
What happened to the nights when the vision was so clear – and I'd look forward to someday?
What happened to my standards? What has become of my life?
Why so much confusion? What happened to my child and my wife?
Why have I made so many mistakes, thinking it would be all good?
LORD, please redirect me…
I'm desperate now, I need YOU. I've messed my life up bad.
Lord, please give it back to me, the faith that I once had!
Who knew that a man would take my trust?
How was I to know, another would take my health?
What happened to the handsome man I was?
What happened to the confidence in self?
I'm tired of pretending now. I'm ready to bare it all!

What happened to my office? What happened to my call?
What happened to the power – that once worked in me?
What happened to the anointing that set the captive free?
What happened to my life? Disobedience will take you down!
Re-Anoint me Lord and carry me. Let me earn my crown!
I need my name to be written – in the Lambs book of Life,
Never to be erased Oh GOD. Help me to make up my mind,
to be willing to pay the price.
In death there is NO ability – to give YOU Your Deserving Praise..
So tell it to let go of me, so I can Praise Your Name.
What happened to The Visions that use to be so plain?
What happened to that time when YOU let me see Your Face?
What happened to "my" hearing, because now I barely hear Your Voice?
What happened to the faith in GOD – that knew that I was YOURS?
Why the drugs and the gay lifestyle, that has taken so much away?
Why do I now hear voices, contrary to what YOU say?
It's time to silence the enemy! LORD empower me to take my sanity back.
Deliver me again Lord Jesus from smoking a terrible drug called crack."

"What Happened" (2008)

Another miraculous deliverance took place, just by sitting down at the computer and pouring my heart out to the Lord in writing. It was a blogpost on myspace.com originally. I sat there; nothing rehearsed and just poured out of my heart. What you just read is that 'moment' unfolded in a matter of moments / one setting!

All seemed to be well but in 2010, I started doing powder cocaine with two of my "friends"; one from the original group, and

another who came into our brotherhood a year later after our bond formed in 1996, whose name was mentioned already also.
And although Edward and I's relationship was long over, this same year, I would occasionally visit he and his boyfriend's house and snort powder with them sometimes too.

The occasional rendezvous I gave to powder "cocaine" *(which was not really my thing),* gave that spirit of addiction another invitation, and not long after, the following year (2011), I was back to smoking crack, again!

It was on and off, like the first round in 2007, but the fact is, I was on it! It wasn't until I was introduced to Crystal Meth in 2011, that I told Crack bye. And then there was that monster of a (strong) demon to deal with. The Lord set me free from all addiction, Hallelujah!

[We will however revisit this subject in following chapters, for other purposes!]

Initially, I didn't know why my fingers, all of a sudden, begin to tell the-story concerning my past addictions, but I know why. - Now I do! It's a great Segway to the following chapter.

I would live out **my teens** *liking men,* **my early 20's** *losing myself* through disobedience from not walking away from a detrimental relationship when the Lord said it was time. **My mid to late 20's** periodically *on drugs,* (all while knowing God had His Hand and call upon my Life), and **my early 30's** *trying to find me again.*

Part Two: ***THE EVOLUTION***

CHAPTER 3:
"IT's A Spirit!" – ?

CHAPTER 3:

"IT'S A SPIRIT!" - ?

Pre-Chapter Work

You heard *My Story*, but not completely. The piece most important, is yet to come.

Remember those ole preachers I talked with you about in '*The Polar Opposite*' segment of the First chapter? You know; the "abominational's!" – I'm making light of using that phrase but let me be clear: I'm not getting in trouble with the Word, or the Giver of His HOLY Word, trying to please or impress anyone! If the Lord's Word says sex with the same sex is abominable before Him, you can stop looking for me to discredit that. But as I've shared before, there are a lot more things abominable to the Lord according to scripture than just that; (same-sex sex).

But what we need is a case of **what's What('s)** *for all involved, to gain proper understanding to "what" applies to whom, and how! - To the church, (as alluded to in chapter one), you're not fully wrong, but to the gay and lesbian community, neither are you. There's error on Both parts!*

***

We must make the proper divides to make everything make sense for everyone here involved: The **LGBTQ** and **D**ownlow, the **Church**, and the 'I', as in Individual self: - [for the specificity of you who's reading this, in other words]! (This is general knowledge for our community to apply, but the Lord will slightly deal with us differently as individuals. - BUT it; *(the specificities the Lord will bring into your life for your journey, for what He has for you and what He has for you to do)*, will never be given with or as, an occasion to simply *[live in]* sin.)

Thus, permit me to spend some time setting this up.

Consider this really quickly though:

See it's this simple; If God has a problem with a man and a woman having sex with one another if they're not married, how can we reconcile to think that same-sex sex, is ok separately? (Even the natural/original order of sex is forbidden before the Lord without marriage, but two men, "doing it" or two women are alright! – NO. It is not!

Let's jump back in.

Well, what I didn't tell you, is that the same people who point out that same-sex intercourse (before the Lord) **is** an Abomination, are accustomed to declaring, while strongly and whole-heartedly believing, that for two people who are the same gender: to have a liking for one another *(no matter how you flip it)*, that those individuals are invaded with an evil or unclean spirit....

You'd hear them say: "IT'S A SPIRIT", and I can almost guarantee you that if someone is using that term, then in the same breath, the following statement will be: "AND IT NEEDS TO BE CAST OUT!"

SO AGAIN, I'm here to help them out too, because they don't know any better. Yawl Ready?

First: If the preacher said that two men or two women having **sex** with one another is an abomination, then according to the Holy written Word of God, they are right.

> **Leviticus 18:22 Amplified Bible (AMP)**
> **22 You shall not lie [intimately] with a male as one lies with a female; it is repulsive.**

But that's not what they mean when they say it. To them, on the outside looking in, it is all inclusive. IF there's any aspect of an attraction or liking for someone of the same gender as oneself, then again, to them:
"IT'S A SPIRIT, AND IT NEEDs TO BE CAST OUT!"
point blank period.

But that is **not true**.
We have a way to go, so for now, let me just say it this way

THE SIN IS IN THE SEX!

Which is only one factor, because remember,

> *St. Matthew 5:27, 28 (KJV)*
> *27 Ye have heard that it was said by them of old time, Thou shalt not commit adultery: 28 But I say unto you, That whosoever looketh on a woman to lust after her hath committed adultery with her already in his heart.*

So, the sin is also in the "lusts". But you were born as a person; a living soul!

You are not *sex*, and you *(yourself)* aren't *lust*! - Keep that in mind for where we are going!

(Real quick. I'd like to mention a time when I was a younger man, and I had a conversation with my grandmother.)

She was the most vital person to my development to help shape my life on the foundational level of how a child is raised, but as we all aren't, she was not perfect, and the church in the era she came up in, had some things that weren't properly interpreted: such as believing the sabbath was Sunday. **It's Saturday!** *Well anyway, the church of old may have misunderstood a few things scripturally, but you couldn't deny that they had found the true and living God. The church that I experienced as a child; going to church with my grandparents, great aunts, and my mother, had power, which only comes from having actual relationship with the Lord. Today's church has increased in knowledge, but where is the power? In other words, true relationship. '?'* - However, I digress!

Concerning Leviticus 18:22, let's look at the *King James Version* before proceeding; the one I'm most familiar with and / the one my grandmother read from. – It says:

***Leviticus 18:22** (KJV)*
"Thou shalt not lie with mankind, as with womankind: it is abomination"

So again, according to scripture if someone lies intimately / sexually with someone of the same gender, its abominable to God, I.E., Sin.

That is why I make the claim of the *sin being in the sex* itself! In other words, there's a scriptural trail as to why we can say this thus far. – *I'm not just coming up with some slogan!*

(My grandmother literally thought that implied *(also)* that two men were forbidden to sleep in the same bed, period. Let me give you an example. *If two male cousins spent the night with each other, or a male child spent the night at his other male friend's house, other accommodations must be made if the two were supposed to sleep in the same bed. It didn't matter if it were two innocent male children, they couldn't or weren't supposed to do it* - is how that was interpreted. And there may be some who believe that. But let's reel it back in!)

I recently discovered something that Jesus said that I found interesting while we're on this subject. In **Luke 17:34** the Master says:

> "*I tell you, in that night there shall be two men in one bed; the one shall be taken, and the other shall be left.*"

Now what He's talking about is what we call the "end time", at the exact moment that the Lord brings about a separation between those who will be kept as His, and those who will be separated from Him and destroyed!

Which means *"two men in one bed"* shouldn't automatically imply perversion, or that sin is going on. I do believe that men can have a level of intimate energy for one another, and it not be homo-erotic *[sex],* or the other identifiable sin *[lust],* in the equation! –

Jonathan and David's Souls were "knit" together, and he loved David more than a woman, *(1 Sam. 18:1; 2 Sam. 1:26),* yet the prophets have spoken as the mouthpiece of GOD that David was the Lord's righteous and was found pleasing in the sight of God! Now don't get too comfortable because we're still on our way to deliverance!

So, it's interesting that if two men can be in the bed together, *(first, that shows that - with that being the case, in any case, it doesn't have to automatically imply a perverted version of the matter, that 'some sexual anything' is going on),* and one was saved and another was not.

Then what if the two men were even in bed with some level of interest and one *(or both)* of them was the cause or reason that it wasn't carried over into a sexual or perverted situation; obviously one of those two men in the bed was found acceptable to be with the Lord, and the other, not so much?! How is that possible?

Because God judges the heart. ~ *1 Sam. 16:7* Yes, but after the heart, deeds do follow. – Repentance, and action unto Obedience!

So, if your heart *(the Lord judges)* is the type of heart of what you're saying it is, then your deeds will reflect it.

> *"**If** you love me,* (you will) *keep my commandments."* - *John 14:15*

***

Humanity Isn't Sin

At the time I'm writing this book, I do not have a conflict to say without any shame or guilt, that I could embrace or cuddle with a man, and for me; (emphasis on "for me") it wouldn't be anything sexual about it; neither physically, nor mentally, such as in my desires for physical gratification.

But I've had years of practice to walk this out also, and plenty of slipping up before I got here!

Some of you can't do that just yet without it becoming an occasion to sin. But for me, because the Lord has already "delivered" me from the perversion and lust of it, and because my heart is pure in that regard, I could do that, and it still not be a snare! But there's another factor to include and consider here!

> I Corinthians 10:23 Amplified Version (AMP)
> *All things are lawful [that is, morally legitimate, permissible], but not all things are beneficial or advantageous. All things are lawful, but not all things are constructive [to character] and edifying [to spiritual life].*

Just because I "could", doesn't mean that I loosely "should" either; *for what?* Because I've learned that, just because of where 'my' spirit sits in God, doesn't change the risk of what the other person's thoughts or intentions may be, nor does it change the fact that I still have the physical body to crucify, and if given the right / wrong settings and factors, my flesh could be set off too.

I could also confidently say, using the *hypothetical* above as to *slipping up* in such a way, that if so, it certainly wouldn't be intentional. I'm simply saying/acknowledging that I am not above reproach. But by God's grace, His governing Word, and empowerment of His Spirit within me; I do not, nor do I even desire to, "practice sin". But the "factor" that we're talking about here is, why put yourself through things unnecessarily. – Save your energy for slaying demons, not having to rebuke someone for trying to touch you inappropriately while cuddling, *hypothetically speaking!*

Which is why, if I were/did, it would've had to be with another "man of God" who understands where the lines lie that can't be crossed without it becoming sinful. Which in my experience, aren't many at all, which is why this material is necessary! Too many "men of God" living no differently than the heathenistic-based practices of this world.

Living in the realm *(and [lower] vibration)* of **1 John 2:16***(KJV)*.

- Look it up!

***

In the spirit of "what's what", we're closing in and will soon discuss, – *(as promised in previous chapter where we abruptly left off, concerning addictions)* the breakdown *in short form*, of *what IS and what IS NOT a spirit*.

Finally, and speaking of previous chapter, we are finally ready to revisit *My Story*, the untold portion!

To keep us on track, we're transitioning from the church's belief that if you are same gender *interested*, *attracted*, or *loving*, that those persons have an unclean spirit in them, *"and it needs to be cast out!"*, - to what awaits us in the following!

Pre-chapter Work, end here.

It's A Spirit! - ?

The Beginning of Understanding

So. My *then* best friend *Leon* and *I* had similar Christian backgrounds in that, while we were both young, *(although I grew up in the Holiness Church, and he, another)*, we heard and believed the same things in our youth. I can't say what his experience was or if he had already knew of his same sex attraction by the time he heard it first preached or not, but for me, before I even knew I was or would become attracted to men, I was exposed to this belief, which is that anyone who is a 'homosexual' or lesbian, is possessed with a demon, or "unclean spirit".

This is what I was taught from church; (not home).

(Not that "home" didn't believe or understand it to be this way also, but there was a difference. - I saw love at home. I saw hate [on this subject] in the pulpit!)

I believed it, and there was no disputing it. I just knew that this was correct! Well! Because of my best friend and I's similar background, (although we started off as temporary boyfriends for about a month or two and then switched to becoming friends, *as mentioned previously)*. As friends over the years, we always encouraged ourselves from one to the other.

We were best friends. We talked about boys, who we liked, etc. But we Always would circle back around at some point and tell each other, we know that this is wrong, and (guess what), that we needed to be delivered! Now when we said it, I guess we had somewhere in the back of our heads the idea of what was painted for us, before these feelings ever manifested in my Life personally from early church experience, which is: If I can confess that I needed deliverance, and believed what was taught through certain doctrine, then what I was saying without having to spell it out, was that I was filled with some unclean spirit and that it needed casting out of me.

Leon and I met in school, in the Fall of 1996. I was 15 about to be 16, and he had just turned 15 four or five months prior. For two decades we were besties. But of course, not without some bumps in the road.

Here's what I'm getting at. From ages 15 and 16, up to our mid 20's (one decade), we sang the same song to one another. It wasn't a song of me trying to convince him to change, or him doing so either. But every time we had these conversations, it was due to he or myself, coming to the other about our own selves and expressing our feelings and sometimes *frustrations,* about what we were dealing with internally. Knowing in our minds we were living wrong with our same-sex practices according to what we knew, or thought we knew at the time. If it were I, he'd jump on board and share he's been dealing with the same or similar things, and vice versa. It seemed we were synchronized in this regard and encouraged one another when those moments did occur.

Again, for over 10 years of knowing one another, we sang this same *woe is me, we need to be delivered* song to one another. Until one day...!

***

The Phone Call

I was 26 years old at the time, and the phone rang. Who could it be calling? Leon of course. But this day, something was different. On this day, the "song" had changed! After whatever preliminary's we went through when I first answered, He then said to me:

> Leon: *"You know what Deon! – I don't believe this is a spirit. (a few other words went here). I believe this is who I am!"*
> *With a big bright lightbulb going off in my head, I'd respond*

> Me: *"You know what! That makes sense. I'm not out here being promiscuous; I'm not out here sleeping around with different / (a lot of) dudes. I just want love with one person."*

The conversation furthered, and we had finally arrived at the epiphany. - That was the day we freed ourselves from that bondage. But that was also the day I was set on course for my **deliverance**, and without even knowing that it was about to happen for me suddenly. That was the moment I thought I would be liberated to be who I was; "a gay man", with no boundaries to the *Word of God* concerning that subject, but the Lord had a totally different plan in mind. The LORD literally took what was meant for my evil and turned it around for my good, instantly. –

We're almost there now.

But first allow me to draw your attention to a few words that are very pivotal. Leon says: "I believe this is **who I am.**"

Because this is the place that everything you read before now, was preparing us for. Let's digress once more! And I'll deal with why I was led to include my past experiences with drugs in the last chapter entitled, My Story.

***

It's a Thin Line

By now I'm sure you've figured out where I'm going at this point. But if you have, it's only *a means to an end*, not the **end** itself: A prerequisite on a major scale. So, stay with me!
So why did the preachers think that who a person was, was a demon in them instead? Because in most cases, it was!

Just as with my past addictions (which was a spirit), there was a means, or portal used to give 'said' spirit access into my life. That portal was the substance itself: (cocaine, methamphetamines)!

James 1:15 says, *when **lust** have **conceived**, it brings in/with it, sin. And then sin produces death.*

What I'm saying, is when you open portals, something is bound to come through them. Something is 'conceived'!

For me and for some, it was the experimentation of whatever drug/substance we tried, and upon discovery of its feel and the liking of its high, then there comes the seek for it. And then to seek it, is what opens the door: and now, the *(spirit of)* lusts is given invitation, and with it, it brings the appetite for whatever it dominates.

Right here, try not to close your mind to seeing **lust** *in a sexual connotation only in this instance; but for whatever!*

~ In the earth, demon's give birth too*!*

Don't be their maternity ward!

Can you imagine that some of us have been breeding grounds for demon activity! 'Conceived' in the belly as an appetite when it's really a demon.

                      Jesus. ~ That ought to creep you out!

And so, when I or another's experience with same-sex liking, turns into actions and deeds, then the door to perversion, *the spirit of* (that is), has just been propped open! Dependent upon what you're dealing with, the door might've just been kicked down. Some spirits are stronger than others!

The only problem is that the church who have experienced perverse spirits entered a man or a woman, *(who gave way to it through same-sex sexual practices)*, has made it a one-size-fits-all narrative, and Now Everything related to same gender liking, loving, or yearning, is a "spirit", - that *'needs to be cast out'* by the way. **Well, that's wrong!**

The spirit world is head of the physical world, yes, but everything here in this life is not a spirit.

The preacher's and church-world have had this conception because there is a strong correlation between the two.

And to *not,* or, *if not* having personal experience to this matter, of course they wouldn't know any better!

Your same-sex NATURAL attraction is not *founded*, *built*, or *established* upon a foreign entity entering you.

However, when you engage with the keys, the portals will be opened, and those strange foreign entities; *unclean spirits*, WILL enter!

What are those you ask. The sin is in the sex. Meaning sexual practices, not just intercourse/penetration sex, but overall sex. And the lusts. When that's a part of your lifestyle while liking your same gender, you are in danger of being overtaken by an appetite that you are no longer in control of, because something else has taken over.

#Portals!

Follow me to the Next Chapter!

CHAPTER 4:
HERE'S YOUR DELIVERANCE

CHAPTER 4:

HERE'S YOUR DELIVERANCE

Finally

So here we are, *Leon* and *I* on this phone call, *(2006).*
And this was the moment that changed my Life.

As soon as I hung up the phone. (Did I mention, *"as soon as"* yet?), I heard the Lord speak to me. I heard the Lord instruct me to get my Bible.

He says, *(as the Lord Himself is my witness, this is what happened.)* –
He first says at the close of my phone call after hanging up:
"Let's say this is who you are, and that it's not a spirit."
"Go to Matthew". I did.

He says: **"Go to the Sixteenth Chapter"**, and so I did.
"Read the Twenty-Fourth verse." And yet I obeyed.

THIS MUST BE DOCUMENTED

I did not say, I just flopped open my Bible and my eyes fell upon something that was illuminated randomly. No.

My Master took 'time' out of eternity to speak to me with specificity. He spoke to me conversationally in each of those instances I shared with you on *the page* before. – On God!

(Now, although at this time of my Life, I had read the entire New Testament at least once, but this was not something I ever remembered reading. My natural eyes had obviously seen it at least once, seeing I had read the book, but that's what makes the scripture supernaturally powerful and the eternal "Word of God". He will hide revelation from you until it's time, or until you can handle it, or until you purify enough to receive the mysteries. [Matthew 13:11; Luke 8:10])

The following is what my eyes fell upon in my *King James Keyword Study Bible* that day.

In obedience, this is what awaited me.

St. Matthew 16:24 (KJV)
Then said Jesus unto his disciples, If any man will come after me, let him deny himself, and take up his cross, and follow me.

Immediately after reading Matthew 16:24, the Lord speaks to me again, and says:

"So I'm telling you, 'Whatever' you are; Deny It!"
(Inclusive of "*whoever*".)

Good GOD ALMIGHTY!

Now here is where **Real Deliverance** (for us) takes its shape.

Can I tell you a secret? God is more intelligent than you, more-than smarter than you, wiser than; more strategic, and more bossed up, than you. Besides, it is He who sits high and looks low, seeing all!

Proverbs 16:9 - "A man's heart *deviseth* his *way*: but the LORD *directeth* his *steps*."

[look up the biblical definitions of the words I have in italics to fully understand this scripture.] - It's powerful!

Remember, I thought I was getting off the phone with Leon, liberated to be a "gay" man.

*(And gay is not synonymous to feminine. Most gay men have no desire to be a female or feminine. "D" in LGBTQ+D, is for **downlow**, which I don't agree with, but (I do understand why), and I can assure you, that for every feminine male you've ever seen, there's 3 to 4 times more men who are gay without a drop of femininity in them; including the ones not in the Downlow (DL) category. We won't even count them! Meaning, the masculine / naturally carrying of themselves men, who are gay and are **not** hiding it. There are so many of them! You just might not have asked and assumed not so, based on their manliness.)*

But back to the subject at-hand, thinking I was finally free to be what I had come to terms with. That I am, a "gay man".

What are you saying preacher? Well, I'm glad you asked.

To my **LGBTQ+D** friends and family:

As long as the preachers told you that who you were was a spirit that needed casting out, then you had a way of escape, and a legitimate excuse based on that fallacy to not heed to the scripture. That's what makes this revelation so powerful.

The voice of the Lord has shut down our excuses! *The LORD* shows us that we too are not exempt. For the requirements the Lord gives to walk properly with Him, is for **"any man"**. – *Verse 24.*

It's general and all-encompassing; even to you, my tender *"this is who I am!"* LGBTQ+ dear friend! – The "D" label is still struggling to accept "who I am" for themselves in their lives.

No judgement to you, I promise. - Hopefully, this material has helped to set you free.

Whether you believe you were born this way or another, we see the truth of scripture come towards your community, down your street, and knocking at *the door of your heart!* - **Will you answer?**

Nobody's exempt!

***

ALL

(It is a fallacy and a trick of the Devil for any of us; not just gay and lesbian folk, but for **anybody** to honestly think that there isn't criterion that goes along *with* or *for us* being Saved. Although Christ died for all humanity, there is still a choice on our behalf, if we are to become recipients of that Salvation. - It's free, but it's not without a standard and the "cost" of acceptance.

When you join a fraternity or sorority for example, there are rules and regulations. So is it with anything else that you become a "member" of: From the Military, down to a gym membership for physical fitness! Children of God, we are in the Lord's armed services. We can't be sloppy, and spiritually out of shape! Because we're soldiers! - "in the army of the Lord." *[If you know, you know!]*

Why is it that we easily abide by the standards put in place on our job, at the gym, and everywhere else, but when it comes to **the Creator** of all, *who* gave us Existence, we think we can give to Him whatever we "feel" like giving?

GOD HAS A STANDARD. There are rules, regulations, and conditions, to be a true **child** of God. And they're not egregious or difficult, but they are there to be observed. It is an opportunity to show where your love and commitment really lies. And most of us are committed to our flesh but we expect for God to save our Souls! Speaking of physical fitness, whatever muscle you work is the muscle that grows. We can't honestly **suspect** to 'work' our flesh, [the gratification muscle group], and **expect** the spirit*(man)* to benefit, do we?)

Does this sound familiar to anyone's childhood? - *'As long as you live in this house, you will abide by my rules!'* (?) If not, you've heard it indirectly elsewhere.

> *Matthew 18:3 KJV*
> *"And said, Verily I say unto you, Except ye be converted, and become as little **children**, ye shall not enter into the kingdom of heaven."*

***

Make It Plain

Prior to now, having a preacher ignorantly tell you that the essence of who you are was a demon in you, was your scapegoat for too long, **but now what?** Then, your thoughts might have been: "*well since the preacher doesn't know what he (or she) is talking about*" (with *this particular matter*), then I can take the approach, that none of it applies or all of it is wrong, and that you can *throw all of it away!* - But that's not so. The scripture isn't wrong, it was just in the wrong hands for you. They didn't understand!

> *We see scripture does apply to us now, and how!*

> *Are you **'any man'**?*

> *If you have life, and profess Jesus is Lord, **it applies!** And not just 'confession with your mouth', but denial of yourself.*

Paul said, "confess with your mouth", but the Messiah said, **'deny with your Life'.**
Which one is weightier?!

And maybe that's why we preach more from Paul than we do from the words of Christ:
because it's easier to duck and dodge when you're living off merely what another man (Paul) has to say, because pertaining to "the Word" Himself, there is no wiggle room or compromise. Just simply obey!
- Read John 10:1
Which is why I didn't mind paying a higher cost for production of this material. The only reason of purpose that this book is in color, is to point out those words in red! – To distinguish that it is the Word of the Lord itself. – John 1:14.
(Too many people put the words of Paul, who wrote letters to other men, cities, and churches, to the same esteem as the word of Christ, who is the actual 'word of God' personified. They are not the same simply because they were compiled together in, or 'as' one book.) Paul's writings were letters, the words of the prophets of 'thus saith', and the words of Christ, are the word(s) of **the LORD**)*.*
However, "all scripture" (2 Timothy 3:16) should be reverenced as holy, and given ear to, including Paul's letters, ~ but know the difference!

-

Before now for someone, you thought that the scriptures were wrong. No, they were just taught wrong. So...

-What's your excuse now *'any man'*?

Romans 3:4a declares: "God forbid: yea, let God be true, but every man a liar:"

Matthew 16:24 are the Words of Christ Himself.
So, we're no longer in man's league, where a man can interpret the law ignorantly, but God's. Man has said *"it's a spirit",* having no scriptural basis for it.

Nowhere does the scripture say anything about *same gender attraction* being a spirit.

In the league of God. (Not of *Paul*, of *Timothy*, or any scribe; but the Christ himself - (He) says: There is no excuse, nor is there escape. If you are going to follow me and be my disciple, then I require you to deny yourself. Gay, lesbian, or the likes, and anything outside of same-gender-loving classifications; meaning "straight" people too! We All must deny ourselves and let "God be true" in our lives: more than what our emotions dictate, what popularity of society says, or what any other influence tries to get us to believe. *Catch this;* more than our 'best friends', when they offer an easy way out of having no responsibility to God's statures, simply because this is who they, or [you] are.

It is what the Lord Says!

We'll talk more about what this self-denial looks like, but first, why did the preachers call this thing a spirit that needed casting out? Well, let's make it plain. - Plainer than before that is!

***

Unclean Spirits

No, my natural attraction for the same gender is not a spirit, but: Let's deal with Lust (not the spirit thereof *per se*) but "of the flesh", (*c.f.* – 1 John 2:16), to get that out of the way first.

In **Matthew 5:28**, Jesus says, if a man looks after a woman to lust after her, he has already committed the act of Adultery in his heart.

The English Standard Version (ESV) says it this way:

²⁸ *But I say to you that everyone who looks at a woman with lustful intent has already committed adultery with her in his heart.*

Now although we haven't gotten to the *spirit* of lust yet, I've inserted this here for the sake of clarity, that even if who you are at heart happens to be a same-gender-loving individual, then you too still commit the sin of "adultery" before the Lord when you look at another person lustfully. No matter the *sex*; *[same* or *opposite!]* Remember, *man looks at the outward appearance, but the Lord looks at the heart.* Inwardly, in other words. – *c.f. 1 Sam. 16:7*

1 John 2:16 King James Version (KJV)
"For all that is in the world, the lust of the flesh, and the lust of the eyes, and the pride of life, is not of the Father, but is of the world."

I've only inserted the previous scripture for the sake of further showing that everything **isn't a spirit**, and that as human beings, there is a "lust" that just simply lies within "the flesh".

However, there's a *spirit of lust* as well.

But the main point, is that everything displeasing to God is **not** a spirit, however, when we open the door to certain things, those certain "things" do sometimes come with certain spirits tagging along! [Put to mind Matthew 12:43-45 here.]

"Sin will always take you further than you intended to go", as I mentioned in *the 2ⁿᵈ chapter, - credited to a former Pastor.*

Why, because something else started driving your mobile vehicle; 'the body'. (*spirits*, *other than your own human spirit*).

Soul ties for instance; briefly.

Have you ever had certain sexual boundaries and drew your invisible line to say, "I will never do" (insert "that" thing ___ here) but found yourself doing just that!? That's because at some point you laid down in intercourse with someone who had already opened themselves up to certain things, accompanied by a certain spirit and boom, you were infected. Not with disease or naturally speaking. But something far more *deadly*:

John 10:10a – "The thief cometh not, but for to steal, and to kill, and to destroy:"

You might not have seen it, there was no immediate symptom of the infection, but you were infected with the same spirit that was dominating the life of the person you gave yourself to, or who gave themselves to you! - [In this instance for example].

Have you heard about the gates that lead to your soul? Your eye gate and ear gate mainly! What you watch and what you listen to, and especially what you indulge in, will give unclean spirits, title, deed, and the keys to your belly. Why did I say that, or use the word belly? Because what's the one thing connected to your stomach (literally speaking)? What I'm referencing is an appetite! When an unclean spirit gains access, your appetite for what that spirit dominates will surely reveal itself not long after entry!

***

What If Gay Is Just Gay?

Now let's get to it concerning this same sex thing. And I'll use myself for an example.

So, if I can say to you, that til' this day, although I'm truly Saved, have been sanctified, and baptized in the Holy Ghost with Fire, *as the scriptures says*, that I still notice an attractive man when I see one, then that's the truth. **Not** even **in** a *lust of the flesh* type of way, but in a, this is a part of who Deon is, type of way; I have an attraction for men! And although the Lord has cleaned me up, and I don't have a lustful, or sexual appetite towards a man, I still know that in my heart, there's still desire there. Well, why am I telling you this? To make it plain.

Although this is a part of the **WHO of who I am**, if I had not been washed by the Word of God, and if I did not have within me the Spirit of Truth / the Holy Ghost; if I were without a pure heart in this regard, not knowing any of these things that I'm sharing here with you, **then** I'd be subject (for illustration purposes), to the following of *ifs*.

Let's say:

I'm just innocently having an attraction from my heart for a man. *IF* I were to then permit myself to engage in intercourse with that man, then I will have endangered myself to opening the door to my soul for unclean spirits to enter in, such as:

*The *spirit of Lust* [(not lust of flesh) *but both are wrong*], but an unclean spirit driving my appetite for more of the appeasements of its appetite, unto sexual gratification.

*The *spirit of perversion*, whereas I was just trying it out or doing the basics, now I'm doing all manner of (even more) defiled things, beyond the fact that I'm doing anything sexual with a man / *(same sex)* at all.

Spirit of effeminacy, where I'm no longer just having sex with another man, but my mannerisms and speech and everything else about my identity as a man, changes with my sexuality; ultimately producing a feminine lifestyle and behavior. - The opposite can apply for females, pertaining to excess of masculinity.

Etcetera

The word "Homosexuality" is not once mentioned in the Bible, but it does say an "effeminate" won't enter the kingdom of God. – *I Corinthians 6:9.* Now let's be clear. That doesn't mean that if you're a 'masculine' guy, willfully engaging in sex with another man, that it makes it alright with God, nor does or shall it serve, (channeling the boardgame: *Monopoly)* as your *'get out of hell'* free card either!

The sin is IN the sex! And not just as in penetration / intercourse sex, but the sexual / *(sin practices)* behavior and activity altogether. That's why I'm free to say, yes, I still find guys attractive, but **not** in a *sexual* or *lustful* way!

And **if** I did see them sexually and lusted for them in that way and chose not to do anything with them, I **still** would be **guilty** of the charge before the Lord, *(that's why we got to do some old-school casting out at the altar of unclean spirits as well),* because remember, even **if** it's the lust there for it alone, and no deed that follows, we're just as guilty! - *(Matt. 5:28)*

[Above, I mean the original English KJV 1611 non-tampered with 'Bible', by the way].

-

SO, THIS IS WHY.
(This is where the confusion has come in!)

Why it was easy for the preacher to look at someone like us; *(how some of you are or used to be)*, and say, that it was a spirit behind why we were the way we were/are. It was a truth in partiality for most cases. Why because, imagine the old church calling you or someone up to the front for prayer! If that person had been indulging in that lifestyle, the chances were very high that a spirit or two had gained entry at this point. So, most preachers were basing this off / from their personal experiences. They saw that effeminate spirit dominating that young man's life when he was called down to the altar. They saw that demon of lust hiding in another individual, etc. So, because they were not *given of God* to walk this out personally, such as I (and others *may*) have, and then be entrusted with this revelation; *[those similar to myself]*, then they spoke on same-sex issues on the level of their understanding and exposure.

And that's why it began to be called or identified as a spirit, when at its core, **to the young lady reading this**, you don't love women because some spirit has overtaken you. **To the young man being ministered to right now**, it's not a spirit! I affirm your *identity*... One that you didn't even ask to have!

But, since discovering the **Who of who you are**, if you have indulged in the practices normally associated with same-sex-attraction, then there's a chance and high risk that there might be "a" or some 'uncleanness' attached to you now, controlling your appetites for the things that **does** need to be 'cast out' at this point. Because you may (just maybe), have opened yourself up to unclean spirits that were resting or settled in another person's life you've been **(sexually)** *intimate* with. - *I have to say it this way, because too many people think that intimacy itself is synonymous to sex, and it is not!*

However, once there is Deliverance from those things, if that is the case for any of you. After all of that, *[deliverance on that level from demon spirits]*, don't be alarmed if you still notice a certain type of attraction **still there**. If it's not lustful, or sexual, and you sense it's in your heart, you're fine. God is working on you, and the spirit that was driving you is gone now, once you allow yourself to be ridded of any entity influencing your internal appetite.

The only thing left to deal with is, that **you're still you**. And it's the ***you*** that Christ **then says** to **"Deny"**. – Matthew 16:24.

***

The Landing

A moment ago, I mentioned the *practices normally associated with same sex attraction*. Because no one has ever told you what to do with those feelings and how to deal with being both a true Christian, as well as what to do with these same gender feelings. The only examples mainly given by our experiences were, it being something about or to do with sex or, that this is [Ok], or it's how it's supposed to be expressed! [sex]. This is the reason why this read is a necessity!

I remember years later, after the Lord giving me the power of **Matthew 16:24** through His illumination to me, that He came back and added these words to my spirit; further fortifying this journey for me, saying:

"I Don't Require You to Pretend to Be Something That You're NOT, But I Do Require You to 'DENY' What You Are."

And it wasn't Him saying it to me for me. He spoke it, in reference to this heartache and disgust I was experiencing from so many gay preachers I was coming in contact that with at that time, that was coming at me sexually; truly not understanding or practicing holiness as a lifestyle, not, a denomination!

I won't bull-jive you. I received the initiation of my Deliverance in 2006 from that one encounter with the Lord intercepting the phone call between Leon and I, - But just like any seed...

"The kingdom of heaven is like to a grain of mustard seed, which a man took, and sowed in his field:" – Matt. 13:31

A seed, first must be planted, given plenty of water, sunshine, and then, given time to sprout. This is why I encourage any of you; if you don't have a normal assembly / church that you are a part of, or, *if you are* a part of an assembly that has stroked the beliefs of your emotions that there is absolutely nothing wrong with how you've been doing things, I.E., living *in sin, (mainly because the ones preaching it to you are doing the same things, and likes to feel justified from what they 'feel' is "ok",* then I humbly ask that you sincerely pray and asks the *LORD* to send you or show you the Church / pastor's that He has ordained for you specifically, for your spiritual growth, walk, and development.

It took 3 years from that moment in 2006 where the seed was planted, before it finally budded into fruit / a spiritual harvest! In 2009 is when I begin to start practicing celibacy, which was the manifestation of truly denying myself as the Lord had told me He required me to do *three years prior, by that experience.* That is why having a church home is vital. Because just as my going to church and hearing the Word of the LORD on a regular basis was watering my seed, so should you, pertaining to this information and your overall personal & spiritual development!

To someone, this is completely new, and thus serves as your *planted seed* sown. Jesus said in scripture, that *the seed is the Word of God,* and thus you will now need to stay in a place where the preached and taught word in your local assembly is going to water your soon coming crop *[this revelation],* so that you too can produce!

- A harvest of what this seed I'm releasing here *to you* produces.

To another, the Lord may have already been dealing with you, and there were some missing pieces to the puzzle that the Lord is now using this material to supply those answers to/for you on some level. And thus, this message may be serving as the *watering* to that which was formerly seeded and planted into your spirit already from elsewhere.

***

Give me the Meat

Someone may be asking, where is this deliverance I was promised?

Well, it's simple actually! It's sort of already been laid out. However, look at it this way. When baking a cake, you not only need proper ingredients, but you also need accurate measurements as well. SO HERE IT IS, spoken more plainly!

Your base is understanding where you're starting from. As mentioned, everyone didn't find themselves in same sex practices or likings, for the same reason as another may have. You may not be as far in*(volved)* as other's are, for some of you. One may have had a college experience, while another; it was just *you* all along. So, let's bake this cake, *i.e., look at it* from the lenses of the *'this is just who I am'* example and perspective.

* To those whose experiences are different, I firmly believe you'll be able to follow along, and find where/how to apply understanding of this, to your situations. *

On your journey, growing into adulthood usually means that you are also growing more into yourself. Here's why there's so much hypocrisy in the church with people who are in leadership, as it pertains to sexual immorality; particularly of the same-sex kind in this instance. Not ignoring that it's just as bad in the overall church as it relates to fornication and adultery for heterosexuals too.

- However, that, is not our subject.

So, some of you, again, who discovered who you are; you grew into yourself as you grew into adulthood. However, what tends or has tended to happen is when your cake was baking, i.e., *'your', coming into 'self'*, there were ingredients and processes that you were **unaware** of, so by default, they were left out of the recipe.

Here's an example.

If you spent the majority of your life noticing, and then liking *(being attracted to)* the same sex, you may have also been one of the ones early-on, who did your *due diligence* according to your perceived understanding at that particularly time of your life, - And prayed to the Lord, even earnestly, that the Lord would "deliver" you, and take that same-sex-attraction and *(those)* feelings away! When you discovered that He never did, that became your further proof, that *"this is just what it is!"*, and therefore you settled into that mentality that all is well and learned to live your life on those terms.

Where's my deliverance you say!? – Well, again, when your life cake was baking, you came into this, - *this is what it is* status, but without all the ingredients available to you, needed within the equation. And usually, that's where the error comes in at. Particularly [for] preachers who are same-gender-attracted and loving! Since you then discovered that's just who, or a part of 'who you are', you didn't understand, there are still guidelines, therefore, convictions eventually left, and it became ok with or for you to "play around" with other *men*, - and other women, *ladies*. It became the norm!

Because Afterall, you were just doing **you**; what's the harm in that, right? - EVERYTHING!

And *to whom this may concern,* I say this:

(Mostly to my fellow preachers)

And that is how *you* became a hypocrite.

Because to preach *God* and live according to the *flesh*,
is indeed hypocrisy!

Well anyway, and *to whom*, it's not altogether your fault(s). When our lives began to bake, we didn't have the actual full and proper recipe. Again, and here it is. = MATTHEW 16:24, and rightly divided - There is a responsibility to anybody, (*not just preachers*) who call or consider themselves to be *Christian, Followers of Christ*, (even to those of us who are the true *Israelites*, and so on), **to deny yourselves** of you, *(no matter who you are, and what you discovered concerning self)*, if anything pertaining to **you** is direct opposition to the will and word of the Lord.

Again, pertaining to this, it doesn't mean you are obligated to pretend being something else honestly, but holiness is a part of the package of living for the LORD your God, no matter who you are.

Remember I shared this with you. The Lord said to me these exact words once before:

"I DON'T REQUIRE YOU TO PRETEND TO BE SOMETHING *(that)* YOU ARE NOT, BUT I DO REQUIRE YOU TO DENY WHAT YOU ARE."

***

No Man Builds a House

(Referencing Luke 14:28)

To properly deny yourself in the way that the Lord means it, requires some building, and nothing's built without the proper tools! There's no sugar coating or finding some smooth way around this. The "tool" you're going to need, is the *real*.... Holy Ghost. You must be baptized in the Lord's Spirit, to have the power to apply this longing that God has for you, for real.

Let *the Lord* minister to you on this factor as you go forth with your lives after this point, but I'll give you a few pointers here to hopefully help. In the church world, we used to more often use a word called *sanctification*, which simply means *to be set apart*.

All I know, is that before I received the Lord's Spirit coming to live *inside* me, there was a preparation that took place, although I didn't know at the time that-that is what I was being prepared for.

The Lord needs to get you in a place by yourself to sanctify you. That means, He'll begin to *perhaps* tell you to pull back from your friends, or certain friends. Perhaps, He'll have you stay home more often than you're accustomed to. These are a small number of processes the Lord uses to begin to dig things out of your inner man, as He is preparing and making room for the Holy Spirit to come in and dwell within you! It's a spiritual cleaning, in other words.

The Bible tells us that the Spirit has been 'with' us already, but it is a major difference from having Him around, to having Him live inside.

*The Spirit first comes 'around', to *clean*. – *1 Peter 1:2*
*Then He comes 'inside' to live. - *John 14:17* (c.f. 7:39)

He is the tool that you're going to need, to *'build up your most holy faith'*, - c.f. **Jude 1:20**; the *Spirit of Truth*, that you might apply and live out these simple guidelines. If you truly ever come to love the Lord, you'll see just how 'simple' these guidelines really are.

***

Get Your Weight Up

Also, let me explain why some people who have at some point been baptized in *the Holy Ghost/Holy Spirit,* and can possibly STILL live-in sin. In 'sin practices', that is!

For some reason when I was younger, I used to think the Spirit was more powerful and authoritative than the Lord's word.. A misdiagnosis of the ranking of the Holy trinity!

Earlier, I alluded to and mentioned **John 1:14**, which says:
14 And the Word was made flesh, and dwelt among us, (and we beheld his glory, the glory as of the only begotten of the Father,) full of grace and truth.

But "in the beginning" it says this!
1In the beginning God created the heaven and the earth.2 And the earth was without form, and void; and

*darkness was upon the face of the deep. And the Spirit of God moved upon the face of the waters. – **Genesis 1:1,2***

I believe this is mainly why / where I got the idea earlier on in life that "The Spirit" was weightier. But I learned over time, things such as **Matthew 10:40 (KJV);** (a conversation between the Master and His disciples, where He says):
40 He that receiveth you receiveth me, and he that receiveth me receiveth him that sent me.

Scripture speaking in reference to whoever He sends and has commissioned, that, to those who receive them; (His disciples), they automatically receive(s) Him, for He is their head, and it is His authority that they've come in to begin with, *to whomsoever they come.*

Look at this, for a reference point!
3 But I would have you know, that the head of every man is Christ; and the head of the woman is the man; and the head of Christ is God. – I Corinthians 11:3 (KJV)

20 Verily, verily, I say unto you, He that receiveth whomsoever I send receiveth me; and he that receiveth me receiveth him that sent me. – John 13:20

JOHN 16:5-7
*5 But now I go my way **to him that sent me**; and none of you asketh me, Whither goest thou?*
6 But because I have said these things unto you, sorrow hath filled your heart.
*7 Nevertheless I tell you the truth; It is expedient for you that I go away: for if I go not away, the Comforter will not come unto you; but if I depart, **I will send him unto you**.*

The Father sent the son because HE is His head. The Son / *The manifested Word of God* sent the Spirit because He, *the Word of God*, is the head of the Spirit.... WHICH MEANS!!!
The reason some of you got the Holy Ghost and STILL can't live right, is because His headship is out of place in your life. In order that the **Spirit of Truth** functions properly in ones' Life, the Spirit must be subject and connected to His Head / the One that

sent Him, in order to be about His (the Word of God's) business. JUST as the Word of God came to be about His FATHER's Business, which is His HEAD. *[Luke 2:29]* You know, the One that sent Him!

So, if my life and my inner man doesn't have the Word of God in me, governing my Life, then of course the Holy Ghost (in me) will be dysfunctional and disproportionately working, because the Author and Headship of *the Spirit*, which is 'the Word'; *(not just lip service and my ability to quote it)*, isn't adequately in me!

Reference Matt. 7:21
*[and that's not me blaspheming against the Holy Ghost, that's me pointing out to some of you, YOUR Abuse **of** His presence!]*

For, to quote the word, compared to having it (working) in my heart is not the same thing.

When I take the Word of God seriously, I give the Holy Ghost something to **move on** and to work with, because remember, in Genesis 1:3 when the Spirit moved upon the face of the waters, He was moving to the command of The Word of God; proper ranking! When the Word is where He ought to be in your Life, then you too, can experience the Holy Ghost for who *He* really is,

A teacher and guider; One Who brings you into All Truth.
- **John 16:13**

He, *(not "It" - v.13)*, is NOT tongues *(only)* and a run around the church. He is certainly not in *some* of this dancing we are doing, full of performances of the flesh! – I hate to say it this way to whom it applies, but: Sit down and get real [first], so you can have something holy to *holy* dance about!

He comes as your "get Right!"
So, give Him some *Word*, to get you right!
The Holy Ghost moves on the Word, and there's not enough word in any of us who received the baptism of fire, and still living in sin!

***

The (c)ross

[As promised from earlier / on the matter of denial of self.]
I suppose it would help if it were made clear what it means or looks like to "pick up your cross". Essentially what's to be interpreted is that your cross is something 'heavy' in your life that you have to

carry. It's mostly internal, which means there's no luxury of leaving it home sometimes so your load might be lighter and better that day. It goes with you everywhere; *or should!*

A person's personal cross varies from one individual to another.

For example, *there are some* who have kidney failure and thus, their Heavy-Life-Load is having to take *dialysis* treatment; *a process where a person's blood (on a machine) is pumped out of his/her body. - With a chemical mix, the blood is then cleansed from toxins the kidney no longer does naturally, and then pumped back into their bloodstream. – [Participants are confined to this process three days a week, usually.]* Having to repeat this process all their life, *(if not for a transplant)*, is what qualifies this instance as an example. It's perpetual. It's heavy! It's an inconvenience to anyone who has such a cross in their lives to bear.

The word of God happens to be using a more inner personal trait when it's mentioned. And of course, there's spiritual implication! Such as personal stances and developments of self.

For instance, having hoped to have painted a well enough picture of what bearing a cross in your life might look like; I say on! – Some of you (us); although on the surface will seem to others as Minuit, but **some folks' crosses** **are simply who they are**.

No one asked or sought out to be gay! And contrary to heterosexual belief, we weren't molested by anyone either that caused us to initially find interest and attraction in the same gender. Of course, not being insensitive. I am aware that many have unfortunately, been victimized in such a way. And to you, I empathize, and I stand with you for your healing from such scar!

Some of us had no childhood traumatic experience, and just simply discovered ourselves, which happened to be same gender attracted individuals. And so, for you: simply who you are, is your cross you have to bear! This one is seemingly more difficult than the instance I mentioned moments ago. Well, how so? The example I gave was an instance of circumstance that occurred at some point in the person's life, which we don't deny is most certainly 'heavy' and life altering. However, what about when your cross is simply you!?

V.24b - "deny himself, take up his cross, and follow me"!

Ok, when having to deny yourself, the cross becomes, placing a greater demand and value on what God says, whether than what I say. Which really means, my cross is simply the denial of a part of 'me' – and me, I can't escape. "Me" isn't a circumstance that eventually happened to me that altered my course. At no given time while alive, have you and I ever been without, (nor can I get away from) the person of "me". And that's what makes it an even heavier cross because it is above or beyond circumstantial. God's word says I can't be me; *not the version I would've settled for,* if what happens to be 'me', is contrary to His command and His way!

And this is what I mean for you concerning "Real Deliverance". If you are sick, that is circumstantial, and you can be healed from that sickness through the Spirit and Power of God. If you are diseased, you can be freed from that spirit of infirmity. And many other circumstantial situations! But deliverance from *me*. That's another angle!

Understand "circumstantial" as being, *not being born with this, (whatever 'this' is). And if by chance I was born with it (a man born blind, for instance), that's still not the normal function of the eye.* Its purpose for you is to see out of. And that's why it was no super-duper deal to the Messiah to 'open up' *(bring sight to)* blinded eyes, because the eye was created to be opened and saw-through in the first place!

But if you are you, what is God delivering you from? - In the sense of there being something wrong that's needing correcting! (Like the Ear that was made to hear, but s/he who happens to be deaf) - Therefore, **this is where the differentiation comes in**.

For a person who is simply who they are - compared to - circumstantial situations, where miracles simply come to correct something to function as it was originally intended. Then this deliverance for the *Lesbian, Gay, Bi-sexual, Transgender, Queer*, and/or even *Downlow* person, is not that same process! What deliverance for us is, is being loosed from the sin *(that normally accompanies our world)* that we've found and have become entangled in as a result of us exploring simply being "us", [when formerly not knowing how to be the versions of ourselves that doesn't displease our FATHER; when all the ingredients to your cake are added]. - Your *real deliverance* is NOT, *"I don't like men no more!"* fellas. Neither is it, that you're supposed to no longer acknowledge another handsome brother when you see one. [AND I AM NOT SPEAKING of LUST *(You do need that other type, if your mind and spirit, and entire life is perverted)*].

Our deliverance is not being knocked in the floor and you get up and supposedly, you're no longer YOU no more. OH MY GOD, are you hearing me people? For your situation, [not circumstantial], but to *"this is who I am"*, you and I's deliverance is in *1)*, [this prerequisite], *Not* pretending that you're not who you are, and then, *2)*, when everything about *who you are (that keeps you outside of God's plan)* is brought subject, and you're no longer disqualified nor *kept from* His will any longer! That's real deliverance. Not me, 'not being me'!

For example, me still seeing another guy as attractive is not me needing deliverance. If my life was not governed by the Word of the Lord, and I did "me"; *my own thing*, - then I need delivering!

***

The Tool!

My deliverance came when I was freed to know, there isn't anything wrong with me, being who I am. I didn't ask for a part of Deon to see a dude, and there be something about a guy that I liked.

When that part of my Life no longer dictated to me that I had to see guys lustfully and sexually; having to indulge in those things, when that *changed*, and in place of / in its stead, there was given me a power to acknowledge an attractive man, but nothing pulls me into sin. That's a level of deliverance for us.

Having power in this world to not be a slave to the *nature of man*, which is the *slave to sin*, [since the Adam/Eve, *Genesis 3:1-24* "Fall" occurred], then, outside of the Lord's saving grace: You must receive the baptism of the Holy Ghost to receive this power to no longer be a slave to this world's system. There is no other way. And if it were, it wouldn't be worth going through the extremities. He helps you with what you could never do on your own, and with ease! Glory to God our help!

You need the Holy Ghost; (to **build** this temple of God in earthen vessel, especially to bear this type of cross!)

Not the organ ghost. Not the tune-me(up)ghost. And not the emotional ghost, because the Real HOLY GHOST is not a dance. He is the Spirit of *Truth* that leads you into all of that; the *truth!* – [John 14:17, 26; **16:13**]. And again, the real Holy Ghost, when He does dance you, if He does, (and he does for some of us), we'll know it's real, and see the difference.

God wants your body and life subject. More than He wants your tithes, your sacrifices (over obedience), and your services rendered in the church service. He wants you / your heart first!

But the Holy Ghost:

He is *power - (Acts 1:8)!* And not power to '*lay hands on the sick*'. *That's not power, those are gifts. Spiritual gifts!* Scripture says so, according to *1 Corinthians, chapter 12*.

This Power, however, is to help you live Right, in a world full of wrong. That's power!

    Being free FROM sin, although 'you are you',
    Is deliverance for our community!
    The End... Almost!

Part Three: *SETTLED GRACE*

CHAPTER 5:
LOOSE ENDS

CHAPTER 5:

LOOSE ENDS

*MARIAGE: *To Be or Not to Be?*

Let's take it back to beginning. That is why reading *The Introduction* is very important! If you haven't done so, please pause where you are in this journal and do so, then come back to where you left off. So that when I say who you are, you know what I mean, and the staple that it is for what we're doing!

And with that said:

By now you should know that there's a difference between 'Who you are', and the mutated versions of 'self' we turn into via *our sin practices* and demonic entry, beyond where "this is who I am" starts and stops. We now know that they are not one in the same! We know this much, but where do we go from here?

My brother's and sister's! True deliverance is a complete inside job. There is nothing external we should look for to determine or base that from, but only by the condition of the heart.

1 Samuel 16:7 King James Version (KJV)
"But the Lord said unto Samuel, Look not on his countenance, or on the height of his stature; because I have refused him: for the Lord seeth not as man seeth; **for man looketh on the outward appearance, but the Lord looketh on the heart.***"*

That's where it begins, and where it all takes place. If it's real at least! Only true internal change produces the following, listed below; *[external factors included.]*

II Corinthians 5:17 (KJV)
Therefore if any man be in Christ, he is a new creature: old things are passed away; behold, all things are become new.

You're probably tired of seeing this next scripture referenced by now, but this time we've crossed over into another means. Remember when Jesus says if we were to look at another individual with lust, *(where?),* in our hearts, that we are guilty of the act as if we did the deed? - **St. Matthew 5:27, 28 (KJV)**. Well, that's why I can confidently say, the Lord is looking there mainly. It is not enough to wear façades for the church world, or around certain people, when the Lord knows all. Once our hearts are pure, you're ok with God, even when you're still not ok with man and man's approval. Remember, man's still looking on what they can see, but no one knows what's happening inwardly with you, but you and your Maker!

But to be clear, there will be external changes that manifest within anyone whose heart has truly been captured by *the Lord*. The point is, not to be boxed in nor convinced by anyone's thinking, that's where it *(your deliverance)* is, in those external factors!

***

Let God be True

After the Lord took lust out of me, and the desire or urge to gratify a sexual appetite and cleaned my Life up from what I call "the practice of sin", I then was left with the evidence of what Leon and I discussed on that faithful day many years ago; that *"this is who I am!"* All these things aforementioned were stripped from me, which could no longer find any identity with mine, and that is when proof came that *even then,* there was there left still an internal desire to love a man and receive love from a man as well. That's how I knew / *(discovered)* that I was what I've called or described before as being *'homosexual at heart!'* No lust, no sex, no fantasies; just a desire for love. Overtime, during the processes / *steps* of my deliverance, after truly being changed, I was still left with *ME*. The 'who I truly am' me.

    The desire there became a longing for a non-sexual relationship with a man, because who we are, is indeed, at heart. And in my heart, nothing changed! My desire in my flesh was delivered, my deeds were no longer in bondage to sin practices, my mind didn't any longer *'look after a man to lust after him',* but I was still left with the heart of Deon. The "heart's" desire is not a spirit that needs to be cast out, but again, once everything else is stripped from you as the Lord is cleaning you up *on the inside*; once you're stripped bare, down to the "you of who you are", then you apply Matthew 16:24 on top of that.

> *"If any man will come after me, let him deny himself, take up his cross, and follow me."*

    In other words, using myself as the example, it's no matter that, after my spiritual cleansing, and I found that *in my natural man,* I'm a gay man at the core; a *'homosexual at heart,'* as I said before. - H*owever*, I'm a 'gay' man that applies: Anything that's within, *[my natural (who I am) self],* that conflicts with the Lord's will, His plan (for my Life), His commandments, or anything else, and watch this, **even that** which is *not of the sin category* either: if it's my *Abraham being asked to give up my Isaac*; the very thing that the Lord personally delivered to me, if I'm asked to give it up; **sin or no sin**, then that's where I DENY MYSELF in that very thing! Why, because *I am*, as are all of us, are called to Love God first and primarily above all else, even more than oneself, *which means*, I put what God says as the primary thing, even when what He's saying is directly opposing 'me' or how 'I' feel about it. Even when in our own raggedy minds, it doesn't make sense!

In this moment, may I direct your attention to an example of this in the BIBLE?!

Quick story! ***[2 Kings 5:1-19]***

There was a prophet named Elisha, and a king of another nation sent his servant, who was the captain of his army, to the prophet. The captain's name was Naaman! The reason he came to the prophet was because he was a leper and hoped that he'd be healed. When Naaman arrived, the prophet didn't even come outside to greet him. He simply told a messenger, to go out and tell him what to do, which was to go and dip in the Jordan River seven times. Naaman was already aggravated because the prophet Elisha didn't even come out to him. Now he's further frustrated because the instructions were grievous to him.

His argument was, out of all the surrounding bodies of water that are near; the many beautiful clean rivers of Damascus, why would he have me go to the worse river, (in his mind, in comparison). He was offended, and almost ignored the instructions. But someone in his company convinced him to just try it. - Naaman stepped into the Jordan full of leprosy, and after dipping seven times, (like the prophet said), he came out completely healed. Leprosy is what we would consider in modern times, an incurable disease!

My point for sharing this is to paint the picture, that the Lord is going to challenge what you think, how you see things, and your own mind's reasonings. And if you allow your mind to talk you out of what your natural *man* doesn't want to hear or agree with, it will very well be at the cost of your own benefit.

Naaman almost missed his miracle, because it was not in *what* or *how* he saw it, or *where* he thought it'd come from.

> *But God hath chosen the foolish things of the world to confound the wise; and God hath chosen the weak things of the world to confound the things which are mighty; - I Corinthians 1:27*

We know that deliverance is not external; For instance, that me marrying a woman does not "cure" my gayness, and you having sex with a "wife" once or twice; producing an offspring, doesn't transform your life inwardly to what it appears to be externally! I think some preachers are more interested in you looking the part, whether than being the part, *(I say this out of what I consider, a personal experience)*. And being the part is NOT the equivalency of *"I married a woman"*, or *"man"* to the women. And that's where we find ourselves now in the process. We must deal with that!

✳✳✳

I Now Pronounce You Husband and Wife

Allow me to make one distinction first! Just as myself have discovered, *(and some others will)*, that after my spiritual cleaning; *(no spirit of uncleanness influencer there to blame any longer)*, I'm still homosexual at heart, and it's part of who I am, - that by far, it is not one-size-fits-all for everyone!

There are some brothers and sisters of ours who may have found themselves at some point involved in lesbian and gay practices, who are actually "heterosexual at heart" instead! And in those cases, once the word of truth gets in them, and the spiritual deliverances take place from spirits of influence, such as *perversion* [only for example}, *(IF that is the case with any of them, or you, [for everyone is not demon possessed, which is the point of half the purpose of this book, to those who know **no** better])*, then naturally so, after rediscovering and being reunited with their true selves, heart, and core being, then marriage to the opposite sex isn't such a shocker, nor an issue:

To whom this applies; to the *heterosexual at heart*, (who got caught up in the experience at some point), I say this to you: Please, (still) don't rush (it); *this marriage thing,* because you're trying to provide an 'outward' show to your pastor(s), parents, family, or whomever else; *even yourself,* that you've "been delivered", by *the church folk/outside looking in standard.* - That's potentially not deliverance, that's entrapment! Toward or unto yourself and to the person to whom you drag into such a façade!

Please wait on God. – Generally speaking, the Lord placed in my spirit several years ago: Why (should someone) put energy into trying to look the part, when you can BE the part! Real Deliverance is not what they told you or you've overheard them say; I promise! The Bible says that the kingdom of God is within you. *– Luke 17:21*

Once true internal change happens, and you are indeed heterosexual at heart, my young brother, pray as the scripture says, that you find your wife. To my sisters, let him find you, although it is perfectly fine that you ask the Lord to allow the one, *HE has for you,* to find you! Please don't rush or fold to the pressure of wanting to prove to others you've changed, or, as it relates to those of you who aren't found out, for the sake of never being suspected of to begin with. Do you hear me? Don't do it for that purpose either!

One of my former pastors not once ever let me preach, having been there at the church for 8 whole years. I was a minister in that ministry, but you know what the problem was, by way of revelation, I discovered that he was looking for me to have a ring on my finger and a woman on my side, as evidence that I was no longer who I used to be. And that's not God's, Christ's, or the word of God's version; it's man's! - *I'll prove it to you shortly,* **scripturally***!*

Everyone isn't even ordained to be married. I'm talking to heterosexual / 'straight' people here! So how much more does God require a non-heterosexual to marry the opposite sex for the sake of pretense? Ut-oh!

***

The Elephant in the Church

There is a spiritual epidemic in the church at large, and with the similitude of the description of the 2020 world-wide pandemic, (which shall *in this moment* remain nameless), many households; particularly spouses, are coming into contact with this potentially deadly disease, and have no clue!

Earlier I mentioned that I know by experience, that some church leaders, are concerned more with you looking the part, and that's the reason, and from where this 'disease' stems from. - There are so many *down-low brothers in the church*, and 98.999% of them are **married**. And some have children!

The leaders of the church have meant you no harm, unfortunately, most were heterosexual. Now that's not the unfortunate part. However, what is, is that, trying to provide answers for something one is not certified for, will usually do more damage than good.

Let me put it to you this way. If an attorney by profession was given access to the workplace of a chemist and was given the charge to discover a new antidote for the Corona Virus for instance, what do you think would happen? More than likely, he or she would probably blow something up; *(likely the whole laboratory),* mixing the wrong chemicals!

That's what some heterosexual preachers have done to those who are *not*, but who *are* similar to the *'are not's'*, in that their *belief* system; both being *Christian*, are the same, (but) - Given you the wrong prescription! Earlier on, in the last chapter, I told you that prior to now, you had an excuse when the preacher-man misdiagnosed your case, telling you that you were the way you were, due to an evil / unclean spirit that needed to be cast out of you!

Some of the preachers were not trying to give you bad information. But they preach from their profession, I.E., from the lenses as a heterosexual; trying to give you the antidote for that which they have not the skill for and know not of. – So here you have me. :^)

When God got ready to deliver HIS children from Egypt, HE didn't use an outsider. HE took one of HIS children (of Israel) and placed him in the system of what had his people bound: in the house of the Pharaoh, king of Egypt! – This deliverer was not only raised in Egypt from a child - up, but was raised in the highest form, as the grandson of the nation's king. Reared in the palace!

Sidenote: *That's why it's not good to be too quick to judge where people are. There might be someone whose been the chief of sinners. And it just might be, the Lord put them there to learn the inward functions, before HE would release them from that sin, with a know-how for others to now get out also!*

Moses was that man! Pharaoh's own supposed grandson: the one that learned everything about Egypt there could be, *even though he didn't know that it was all for a greater good later,* - was the one that the Lord chose to bring Israel out of Egypt's captivity!

I too hope that the Lord is anointing this material, to bring you out of bondage, from a man who has known it, *this bondage*; first-hand. For, now I can decree, that I am free!

Well anyway, the point is., the Lord is not speaking to you from some *stranger off the street*'s point of view. Neither from the *outside looking in* perspective. Nor am I of another 'profession' trying to guess for you the formula – NO. I am the chemist!

Like Moses, I too have been given an advantage on how to bring you "out", because I was hidden with-'in' all along: In the palace of 'homoSEXual' sin, learning and being shown things I needed to know, when I didn't even know it was happening. Times when I thought I was having a good time in my former drug use and promiscuity, etc.; I was learning lessons that I didn't know school was in session for! But the Lord knew along, what it would take too for me, to also one day say to a thing: "THE LORD SAID - "let MY people go!"

– I speak as an oracle of The Lord in this moment, and it is as if I can hear Him declaring:
The *LGBTQ+D* are "MY people" too.
(They just need to be taught right, but they are still My people!)
Wasn't the former *fornicator*, and *drug abuser*, and *pimp* and *prostitute* already *Mine*, before I cleaned them up and changed them!? - They were already *My* people, that's why they heard my voice *[John 10:4,5,27]*, and came out of those past lifestyles to begin with.
It's time the sheep of this fold receive theirs!

"*Their*, what"?
-Do you hear your Master's voice sisters and brothers!? A **clarion call** is what He'd have you to **receive**. Your way out, and door of escape! Satan has counted on you to be ignorant concerning *his devices,* and the not knowing what the Lord truly requires of those of us who love the same gender as ourselves! There's no excuse now to remain deafened to the Voice of the Lord! Now, we are able to be free from, and distinguish rather, that which can please our Father, *the LORD* God, or not!

So, *the elephant in the church* is due to various reasons.
Well, what is this awkward thing in the room you say; the epidemic of gay and lesbian folk *(at the core and essence of self)* marrying the opposite sex to appear and to appease, and in most cases, when done, it heightened the very thing you tried to cage, and tried to suffocate; for it then comes back *(stronger)* with a vengeance. A hefty price to pay, accepting man's deliverance, rather than God's!

As I mentioned earlier, some preachers being concerned with you looking like your life is "right" and caring more for appearances than your own soul's [actual] safety, is a big problem! Human ornaments we are to some. So long as you look the part, some aren't going to labor to get you right for real. *'Just come and decorate my church!'*

Then there's those overzealous preachers, (which mean well), who have young 22-year-old's being 'encouraged' to 'get married', and that they NEED a wife; putting more emphasis on assuming youngsters can't contain themselves if they are taught that that's even an option. Jesus sure thinks it is, and made it plain that not only is it, but that it is the greater and better portion, to those who can. – c.f. Matt. 19:5-12, (*which is* **the scripture** *whereby* **I said I'd prove to you**, *that what man says about marriage, as if it's some elastic onesie that can fit anybody / one-size-fits-all,* **Vs.** *what the Father says through the word of God. - [And they] are not the same!*)

Rather you are 'straight' as an arrow, or gayer than the tooth fairy, everybody is not ordained/supposed to get married, and that is scriptural facts! Yet, unfortunately not taught.

There is a difference between what the Lord requires, and what man's traditions are, which are binding us and doing more harm than good: to keep up with appearances, in the instances that - that *holy matrimony* wasn't so 'holy', cause God didn't put some of you together; pastor did. Influence did! Mama did! Daddy, and *"son when you gone get married"* did!

Thus, some guys don't get to discover themselves before they take on a wife and start a family extra early in life. I'm talking actual heterosexual men here guys!

So, because for so long, the church world has painted marriage as one size fits all, then the undercover / secretly gay men, are strongly "encouraged" by pastor that marriage is a MUST! (Because again, even if you are "straight", marriage still isn't everyone's portion! And again, not to marry, for the sake of full dedication to the Lord, *(if you can abstain),* IS the greater portion.)

> **Matthew 19:5-12 KJV**
> 5 And said, For this cause shall a man leave father and mother, and shall cleave to his wife: and they twain shall be one flesh?
> 6 Wherefore they are no more twain, but one flesh. What therefore God hath joined together, let not man put asunder.
> 7 They say unto him, Why did Moses then command to give a writing of divorcement, and to put her away?
> 8 He saith unto them, Moses because of the hardness of your hearts suffered you to put away your wives: but from the beginning it was not so.
> 9 And I say unto you, Whosoever shall put away his wife, except it be for fornication, and shall marry another, committeth adultery: and whoso marrieth her which is put away doth commit adultery.
> 10 His disciples say unto him, **If the case** of the man **be** so with his wife, **it is not good to marry**.
> 11 But he said unto them, All men cannot receive this saying, save they to whom it is given.
> 12 For there are some eunuchs, which were so born from their mother's womb: and there are some eunuchs, which were made eunuchs of men: and there be eunuchs, which have made themselves eunuchs for the kingdom of heaven's sake. He that is able to receive it, let him receive it.

Not only that, then you have your parents who start looking at you no later than age 24, inquiring about why you're not married, or dating by now, etc. *The pressure!* This is for straight folks too. But this is why so many gay men are married to women in the church, and are doing whatever else with other men on the side. *The illusion!*

Therefore, and thus creating this breeding ground for this big stinking nasty enormous creature in the church-world; *Pretenders!* It is indeed an epidemic and pandemic within the tenants of our faith most assuredly, because when are we going to start preaching rightly divided texts concerning marriage and stop ruining these young people's lives by making them get married before they've had time to discover who they are in God and what He's calling for, for their lives!

So, we preachers and leaders are to blame for all the married downlow/sleeping around with men-men, that we have (quickly) married off to some of our *women: - [innocent bystanders unto victimization of someone else's illusion!]*

Jesus, we have got to do better! - *THIS* is the thing too big to miss and to pretend that we don't see. It's in our pulpits, music departments, pews, and chairs; pastor's and all!

I don't think a lesbian woman probably feels as much pressure to find a man to marry, to hide her identity, as much as it's happening for men in the church, but I could be wrong.

I for one, am tired of looking at this elephant. It smells of rot! May it die (out of our churches, in Jesus' name). May this material, and material like this; *so long as it's truth and in right spirit; God-given*, give this thing it's proper burial!

And let the people get real, so they can get Real Deliverance!

***

MASTURBATION?

Masturbation (*generally speaking*), is wrong! Why, because, again, on a 'general' basis, it is a matter of gratification of the flesh, **[INCLUDE Pornography here as well,** and see - 1 John 2:16]. Which is contrary to One with a lifestyle after God! This means that in order to please God, one must not be in pursuit of those pleasures, but the denial of the weaker portion of the 3-fold makeup of man; *spiri*t, *soul*, and *body*: **the body** being the weakest; *having no power to deny it's urges on its own.* –

A former pastor of mine would say, "having an 'insatiable appetite'!"

It is the willing spirit of a man (Matthew 26:41) that must overrule the flesh, which is the precise posture needed for *the Spirit of truth* (the Holy Ghost) to come in via His baptism and pilot your 'way' through Life. God's way!

HOWEVER ~ This is a very important assignment, and if God targeted those that He desires to transform into a vessel like me; *meaning*, (having identified that I was gay, but given the formula of what is acceptable to God for one recognized as one that's "gay"), then I must give you the full scope of what He's done in my life throughout this journey *thus far*.

In other words, ... I am not here to play (church politics) with you, but to give you the raw truth, for your help and understanding!

This next portion, I only speak to as a Eunuch, and cannot apply this to any other sector, but to those who have been identified by the LORD as such.

* PLEASE SEE **MATTHEW 19:12 KJV** before continuing! *

Modern day definitions are completely bogus, based on more-modernized history within isolated regions of the world it would attribute to, but biblically speaking, and in its origin, a **eunuch** is not a male of castration!

This is evident scripturally also, when the Master says *"For there are some eunuchs, which were so born from their mother's womb:"* so we know He wasn't talking about castration, at all; period. We must "study" (and understand) "to show ourselves approved!" - 2 Tim. 2:15

I can assure you, I am not castrated, but the LORD "made me", like the scripture said, a eunuch for *"the kingdom of heaven's sake."* And all my body parts work!

What is a eunuch? A eunuch is someone who abstains from sex / sex practices, by choice, or by calling of God, although their bodies work to perform, which is why it's a calling or a choice.
It is a calling. It is a choice to answer, and it is a Grace to do so!

Before now, many of you; *those who are, also,* haven't had an open presentation before you to help you identify what the LORD made you, nor have many of you been able to put a name to it. Well, here I am! I'll be your example. You will no longer be *misplaced, out of place,* nor *unidentified,* because no one represented you in the Kingdom before now. Everyone is NOT called to be married!

Psalm 4:3a
But know that the Lord hath set apart him that is godly for himself:

Marriage is wonderful, and sent by God, but it is NOT the end all, be all. | **Argue with Jesus**, not me; He said it!
See the entire context of Matthew 19:1-12

When I first started my journey of self-denial, and celibacy; taking up my cross *called Deon*, and began to follow Christ for real; *meaning His teachings and applying them*, I had to go through another level of sanctification in this case. And after many years of completely sustaining, the Lord spoke instruction to me in my spirit.
DON'T TRY THIS AT HOME!

As a Eunuch, one who has not been granted, nor called by God to marry! - 'Don't try this at home' because if you are not married, and you are waiting on the LORD for your spouse, then keep on waiting in faith, no cutting corners, etc.

But those who've been given to never marry, who are the LORD's eunuch, which means, there is no waiting period to 'hold out" until 'wifey' or 'hubby' comes, because that's not your portion... this is what happened to me!

The Lord gave me permission to periodically, as He said it, *"release myself"*, with these specificities and with what purpose!

Of course, after years of no sex; no nothing! I don't remember the year this took place, but I remember sharing with you that my celibacy journey began in 2009. So, it was long after that!

The LORD, in more recent years, gave me permission and now permits me, *for the purpose of not being overly backed up,* to release myself, but under these terms:

It must be with a clear mind.

-No visuals. No thoughts of anyone or anything!

-And it must only be done after long periods of time, from the place and 'purpose' of not being backed-up, and not ever for the sake of simple gratification of the flesh! Because remember the scripture just once more; *Matthew 5:28*

If I look after a woman, man, cat, dog; *a potato chip*, to lust after it, I've already committed the ACT of adultery within my heart. Thus, watching porn is forbidden. Ejaculating with others is forbidden, etc. Because remember, there is no permittance nor grace bestowed in that area just for gratification, but **a matter of health concerns for a man who never, ever, ever, releases for years on end!** (Again, you can sustain, until God sends your spouse), but one that's a eunuch, we can't go 60 years and our bodies never release sperm in some way. You will even find that after long months of time, and years, that semen will even ooze out of you when you are performing the simple act of urination! Once done with 'peeing', the next thing that will happen, without any effort, is some semen finding its way out, in small ooze's!

YOU CAN'T JUDGE ME, I HEARD FROM GOD! And this is the luxury He gave to me as a Eunuch who went YEARS without any ejaculation! The sovereign One knowing my heart, and knowing His will, that I was not to marry and be one of His eunuchs, He gave me Grace! And that is the only acceptable thing in the sight of the Lord that I know of, for one who has truly been purified and, that isn't lawfully wedded, to share in a 'bed undefiled' – *[Hebrews 13:4]*

Women, I'm sorry that I can't help you on this one, as to speak to it. I don't know that process! But I can say, if you're just trying to gratify self/a feeling, then that's going to be a NO.

And men, if you still on your way to the example or place the Lord has brought someone like me to, over the years; don't even think about it. Go through your process of purification and sanctification; you're going to have to stop everything cold turkey when the Lord initiates your process to sanctifying you as His, and as holy for real. That includes touching yourself! And only the LORD can come back and deliver to you whatever graces He deems necessary for your walk and for your journey with Him, such as with a forever eunuch, not Pastor Williams! I'm only being candid about my journey. This should not in any wise, be interpreted that I can give you or deny you approval on this matter in your life. Only the LORD! Just as it was the LORD that spoke that specifically to me! Wait on the Lord and let Him direct your path.

***

GAY MARRIAGE!

NO, but let me tell you why!

In my youth (as in my 20's), I despised the thought, the topic, and all that *'the thought'* encompassed. It was just wrong!

By my early 30's, I begin to question if it were "ok" with God somehow. I later found out that it is not *ok*! But during that time in my life when I entertained certain conversations about the subject, I remember hearing the LORD say to me once, ***"I'm not going to let you marry a man. Your call is too great to…"*** - *Sabotage my calling and the people I'm supposed to reach.* - But that was personally about me when I didn't know what I know for certain about it now. But let's talk about the matter in general for a moment, and how it applies to all.

To be honest, this next revelation on gay marriage, GOD didn't come to me and seal the deal on, until the same day I submitted this book's first rendition for publishing, Dec. 29, 2020. Just as soon as it was released out of my hands, the LORD decided to talk with me more and take me further! It was concerning this final piece that I had not intended to speak on, but it needs to be established to destroy the deception!

While in a phone conversation that same 29th night, the LORD's enlightening came to me, and this is how He did it…

(Final Detour)

When the LORD delivered me from sex, and drugs, lust, and every sin of the flesh that defileth the body and the life of a man, He never took away my natural *'desire'* for a man; the *'one'* inside my heart, no matter how 'hard', sincere, or how long (of a time span) I used to pray about it.

That's why, as revealed in chapter 3, we discover that I still identify and acknowledge myself as being a 'gay man' in some senses for that reason. In full transparency, if I could have love mutually with a man, where we share a life together, but with no sinful deeds like sex, *inclusive of lustful thoughts or desires, or any sexual practices of any sort*, and we both present our bodies and lives as holy unto God, but be there for each other in companionship, I'd say **sign me up!** – I'm still 'gay' in my heart. You can't pray that away!

And "God" isn't concerned about that so much as He is concerned with, whatever your lot in life is, in your *flesh* [where He found you], will you give it up; *your will and way, and 'way' of seeing things,* for Him? - That's His concern!

> Like the Messiah in **Luke 14:26 & Matthew 10:37,** When He said you must forsake your own father and mother for Him. He wasn't saying to literally 'hate' and to disown them as a qualifying factor for the kingdom. What He was saying is that *if by chance I ask,* will you forsake anything without limitation for this 'god thing' you profess!? He was saying, *I'm not telling you to, but you must be willing to not keep anything back from Me that I ask of you; even your Mama if I said so!* - In the case that He'd asked, what'd be your response?
>
> Remember Abraham? – **Genesis 22:11,12 KJV**
>
> ¹¹ And the angel of the LORD called unto him out of heaven, and said, Abraham, Abraham: and he said, Here am I.
> ¹² And he said, Lay not thine hand upon the lad, neither do thou any thing unto him: **for now I know** that thou fearest God, seeing **thou hast not withheld** thy son, thine only son from me.
>
> "Peter, do you love Me more than these?" – John 21:15
> St. Luke 14:27 = **MATTHEW 16:24**

But in the case of coming out of the flesh and being a holy vessel as He is holy, that is not an analogy of 'if by chance'. It is required!

Let's get back on track.
"Gay Marriage"

I brought up My 'gayness' for a reason! For me to deal with this topic and how I finally realized it was an absolute no for gay marriage concerning anyone with same-gender desires according to God's standards, I must offer another transparency as the prerequisite as to how it came about; when the truth came to this degree and was imputed unto me.

So, I met a guy online through Facebook last year who lives in another Country. Somehow, we fell for each other, or came close.

(How can this 'man of God' say this? –

Because ***'the sin is in the sex'***, *and 'the lust' which creates defilements, - not in a pure heart who had no choosing or picking to grow up to discover that their intimate heart was geared towards men.)*

Somehow, thousands of miles away and completely across the Atlantic Ocean, I captured his attention, and he captured my heart. The reason being, there was an establishment of who I am in God, what my standards are, and the detail of how God had geared my life for His specific purpose. He understood the cost, and the fine lines my life were required not to cross! He accepted me and my challenges, and I accepted him and his.

Now, back to the 29th of December! Literally the same night, after submitting the first edition of this book, a conversation was had between he and I, and the revelation [that is to follow] was given. Quite simple!

This 2nd Edition was made as an addendum to specifically address gay marriage.

First, let me recall to you that by this time, I had already encountered God in the manner that He told me years prior, that He wouldn't allow me to marry a man, as I mentioned previously. So, the following the conversation I'm letting you in on, - what I said (during that conversation) was not me being serious, yet from a place of love, nonetheless. I never had the intentions nor the desire to marry same gender. Marrying a man has never been appealing to me personally! But of more importance, I wasn't interested in disobeying God either.

One last thing.

The EST time zone in the States where I'm writing from is a six-hour difference to Nigeria when we're in *'Fall Back'* mode, but five-hours during normal *'Spring Forward'* calculation!

This conversation was in December, so it was six hours at the time. At *2AM* my time, now technically the 30th / *8PM* his, and still the 29th, strikingly a conversation ensued which was not the normal type that we would have. John, *maybe out of insecurity* began to complain that I never showed him any interest in a certain way and questioned was I even attracted to him! (?) I think it was difficult for him to grasp that so many people slobbered over him in their desire because of his physical attractiveness, including his physique, and yet the person he was with, was completely opposite! So, my response began by reminding him [from his complaint he had of me not showing him any sexual interest], was that 'I don't live in that realm, and that I'm a pastor; one walking in spirit', saying *"your body doesn't move me to live in the realm of the flesh"*, I then shockingly said, *"MARRY ME. Sex with anyone you're not married to is wrong. You want me to show you sexual interest; Marry me then:"* (*Although he was the one who used to periodically mention marriage, and I would be the one to shoot it down, which is why my words were so shocking to myself,)*

It was in that moment immediately that the LORD illuminated for me and showed me a clear picture instantaneously once those words came out of my mouth. And like autopilot, completely out of my control, my mouth opened and out of it came: **"that is why"**.

John inquired what was I talking about when I blurted it out, but the LORD didn't allow me to share it with him in the moment.

The totality of our conversation lasted to about 7am my time.

Once the conversation ended, I pulled out my phone and texted this experience to myself. These exact words:

Timestamp of Dec.30 7:08AM

"On December 29,2020; the SAME Day I published This Must be Documented, the Lord showed me a clear answer, while on phone with John, *First name, Middle name removed*, what the matter is concerning Same-Sex Marriage. I was telling *removed*, from his complaint of me showing him sexual interest, that I don't live in that realm, and that I'm a pastor; one walking in spirit, *your body doesn't move me, to live in the realm of the flesh,* thus in my response to his complaint and my saying those other things, I concluded by saying, *'MARRY ME; sex with anyone you're not married to is wrong; you want me to show you sexual interest; Marry me then:'*

It was in the moment, the Lord illuminated, and I said out of my mouth, "that is why".

The Lord had just showed me, the area in my book, where I wrote to the readers, that Leviticus clearly says sex between two men is abominable before the Lord, therefore. It's written, and getting married to one, does not UNDO that law of God, the LORD.

I used to say no it's wrong, then I would say at some point; later coming to this, that I didn't know, if it were ok, but just that God said He wasn't letting me marry a man.

But last night; really it was 12/30 during 2 to 3am hour; having this conversation, it was solidified that same sex marriage is No."

Leviticus clearly says sex between two men is abominable before the Lord, therefore, getting married to one of the same sexes is not a scapegoat, nor does it negate. Same-sex marriage does not undo the law of God!

Marrying a man, or *for the ladies*, another woman, is an arbitration and attempted loophole. **John 10:1** says:

"Verily, verily, I say unto you, He that entereth not by the door into the sheepfold, but climbeth up some other way, the same is a thief and a robber."

'Ain't no loopholes bruh! - Not, *'there isn't'*, but 'ain't.'

The standard has already been set. It is sinful and unlawful by the law of God that any two *or more* men, *or women of same*, should perform sexual acts with one another. Marrying one, in essence, is saying *'I found a way around God's standards'*, deceptively thinking the marriage certificate will undo what God's stance on it, already is!

GOD showed me this in the "***that is why***", as clear as day. It was so clear what He delivered to me, why it's unacceptable!

"IT IS WRITTEN".

You shall not lie sexually with a man of your kind", married or not.

END.

This *HAS* Been Documented –
Real Deliverance for the LGBTQ+D.

The

CONCLUSION

Matthew 16:24 –
Prior to that great day at Age 26, those words in the text wouldn't've been anything more than just letters on a page. Don't get me wrong, I had long before then, acknowledged in its entirety *the Book* of the Bible to be a holy scroll, but the aforementioned, simply meaning there was nothing illuminating and Life changing in this text to me, particularly on this subject matter, prior to this moment that day.

The Lord granted and gave me a beautiful personal experience with Him. It was truly supernatural! - I liken it to the *Saul to Paul Conversion* experience. – *(Acts 9:1-12)*. It was of most necessity, for my personal development with Him, for me. So long ago, without my knowledge, the Lord having this *Right Here/Right Now* moment in mind all along! In other words, although I didn't know it, my "personal" experience wasn't so personal after all, as He had you in Mind the entire time. So that, what He is saying, might now become *personal* for you as well.

Thus, as my eyes had to be opened, *(Acts 9:12-18)*, so does yours. I understand that the Lord must be the One Who chooses to give this to you as well! He delights in doing so, which is why He gave me a mandate, to not be stingy with this information Because He has something; a life so much greater for you than what you've been previously bound by. The Lord told me years ago, *and they shall call you Truth Teller*. Well, here it is. Receive it!

Paul was changed by that supernatural encounter forever.

And just as Paul was changed forever, so was I.

Just as I, so be it, you.

Let us Pray!

FATHER, I bring two persons' before you today!
One that's known by experience, and whose struggled to figure it out; *most, who've given in to the idea of "it must be this way", (ultimately no longer striving to please you; settling into a life of hypocrisy, simply by just not knowing),* or either for: believing that they *are* pleasing to You based on 'good deeds' and other 'works'; never truly considering that none of those "sacrifices" are substitutes for "obedience", and thus, are displeasing to You, even if they think they are not.

And *the other*, who has no clue, but has cast judgments on the first set of persons'; *lacking the understanding and compassion of YOUR Love.:* That although YOU are a Holy god *Lord,* and there is a standard, but that YOU still don't think like men. YOU said perfect Love casts out fear, and fear and torment is of the devil; thus, when we use vulgar words from a profane heart to express our dislike for same gender attracted person's, we then become all the more guilty before YOU. As even now, I hear YOUR Word say: *"that in the same manner that we judge, so shall it be measured to us again"*.

FATHER, YOUR Church is divided, although for a variation of reasons, but pertaining to this matter, there is division in a major way. No, this is not an occasion for any of us to sin nor disrespect YOUR holiness, but I ask that through this text, and whatever other means YOU choose, that the heterosexual Christian believer's hearts be touched. Show them the fine line Father God, that it is not the attraction itself, *(unless it's lust)* that is brought before YOU as sin, but rather, the deeds and thoughts from that attraction. Show the "straight" man and woman who says that YOU and Your Love resides in them, how to love those that they don't understand, who are of a different orientation from them within *heart's desire,* **although they have the Biblical right to disagree with the deeds.** ~ Using the word 'orientation' *because it surely isn't preference* and something we can choose to, *not to be!* ~ **Although we can choose to please You despite ourselves, with simply following Your guidelines.**

Just importantly, I ask that **You** show the heterosexual pastor, preacher, and those with such platforms (that lead Your people), what real deliverance for a gay or lesbian person is before Your Sight Lord God. YOU'VE shown us in Your Word, that Your Ways are so much Higher than ours, and so are Your Thoughts!

YOU Called me to write this material to help someone understand, and NOW I ask that YOU Deliver my brothers and sisters all over the Earth from the bondage of sin that's entrapped by way of the indulging, when they did not have Your understanding previously on how a gay man or lesbian woman can still be pleasing to YOU. | Wasn't it YOU Who Said in Your Word, that YOU Desire that not One soul be lost? Therefore, I ask that you help the "straight" folks to understand, that it has never been Your idea or plan to cast an entire type or group of people to hell. The understanding, although lacking, was that they *(those who like people of the same sex)* were supposed to magically no longer be who they naturally are. The belief has been that every one of us whose lived this life, must've been molested, raped, or sexually abused as a child, which is a Fallacy! And, also, that the person's You've made us, are demon spirits instead. Lord help! And because YOU Desire that none be lost, YOU are not interested in a gay man marrying a woman for outward show; *[not loving of her the way Christ has loved us, as scripture says]*; ultimately messing up the sanctity of Your true holy matrimony, preserved for one man and one woman who indeed do love one another deeply; in sharing a forever life together that You Yourself have *"put together"*. Show the Church, I pray Thee, that 'every Christian believer having to be married' is also a fallacy; as Christ told us plainly in the Gospel According to Matthew, in the 19th chapter. ~ That every believer or disciple of Christ is NOT supposed to be married and that it's even greater in Your sight, (as the alternative to marriage), to become one of Your Eunuchs; *(someone devoted to keeping their body from sexual immorality; living a life of celibacy or abstinence indefinitely*, unless at any given time, of Your own free and sovereign will, *You* come and place the desire for the opposite sex in that person and they then marry the person to whom YOU have chosen for them!*)*

I understand that YOU can Do ANYTHING, including, taking out the attraction altogether, but that is in most cases, spiritual manipulation, from *those folding under the pressure of* one's pastor or leader, or even family, and thus pretending that it's gone, when you can never be 'gone' from yourself! - Which ultimately causes (and have caused) MANY to cloak themselves in *unsanctified marriages*, concluding that these *(those types)* marriages are *fake*; thus producing Your people in these cases to be introduced to even greater/increased sin and iniquity in their lives, *by this*, that in addition to first dealing with their struggle alone; being *Single*, **to then** *now* the sin of the act of adultery, as they are now married against their true will, and now, also, keep not the sanctity of the monogamy of marriage, especially when secretly indulging in same-sex sexual practices, while married to the opposite sex! There are some, in some cases who are even marrying, so that they can be advanced in leadership positions in the Christian church, etc., by first off, being taught wrong that marriage is a requirement for leadership!

Deliver these cloaked gay people, hiding behind their wives or husbands, so you can work on the real them; than rather, they have a continued façade send them to Hell!
Help Your entire Church Lord, that we people have messed up in so many ways, as many of us are modern day pharisees, who care for the *"as long as it looks right"* outer presentation, when inwardly, as the scripture says, *we're like dead men's bones!*

I prophesy to the winds, of the four corners of the Earth, to no longer permit disguise to hold back this truth. I prophesy DELIVERANCE for the people like me, *(who unfortunately have not known what to do with themselves)*. That it hit the Earth now, and find them where they are, all over the Earth that is *Yours*, within the fullness hereof! - From Nation to Nation, MAJOR and in-between cities, from villages to small cities; rural and remote. On and off the grid, let your truth for my people, find them in the mighty name of Jesus the Christ. For such a time as this, *LORD,* I thank Thee for preserving my Life, to be entrusted to speak it anyhow, no matter who it offends. For *no liar*, the scriptures saith, *shall tarry in Your sight.* So thank You for making me, shaping me, and molding me into Your truth teller, Jesus. Gather Your people Heavenly Father out of darkness Father God. I give You glory right now! Send this book all over the world, and let it be rightly divided and interpreted, so that no one misinterprets any portion of this material, that to *live in sin* is alright when it is not. Open eyes and understanding, to both *same* and *oppo*site sex loving individuals, who profess You and believe in You.

    Bring it all together for them. And for this I thank Thee Lord, in Jesus' mighty name! And delight in their deliverance; expedite it and see to it that we experience the fullness of You, by the illumination of truth! As much as we are able to experience You in our Human form. Let us come to KNOW and be KNOWN of You Lord God. No forms and presentations of godliness without God, Yourself, being head of our lives!

    Lord I've seen personally, too much hypocrisy in the Church from just this very matter alone. Dry up our stench, like *Yahushua Ha'Mashiach/Emmanuel/Jesus the Christ* did for the woman with the issue of blood. Visit us in our issue; not to destroy, but to save us with Your truth, and defining line of what You will expect out of people like me who can't help who I am, but call on Your name: show us Your standard for us kinds of people, and let not the people turn a deaf ear, to the cry (of You) for salvation (for us), spoken through Your prophet. For I have spoken, as YOU have told me to speak. Let not this prophetic cry and work in obedience I've done for You fall to the ground. I know I am Your true prophet, so let it stand, because I have spoken, because You have told me to do so. In Jesus' mighty high name. Amen.

As we are graced to come into divine relationship with You, in which, everything concerning *life* all about, I thank YOU. DELIVER us ALL; the church at Large! Deliver us from other things, and factors that might be snare to us, and from prerequisite's we need to be cleaned from before we can even process or handle this; to those who have other strongholds keeping them from seeing the reality of what You're saying concerning this subject.

We all need to be washed by You Lord.

I know that a cleaning is coming, for it is scripturally and prophetically declared so, that YOU will receive unto Yourself, according to *Ephesians 5:27*, a church without spot or blemish; the true Church!

We give ourselves to YOU, NOW. And even the things we still don't fully understand, we feel Your presence, and we know deep down inside, regardless of our personal opinions and what it would mean for us - that we'd have to give up to receive this truth, that even if we lied openly and outwardly that 'this is not YOU', we know in Spirit and within our heart of hearts, that it **IS**, You Lord of Host; **The LORD** is *Your Name* according to *Amos 5:8* and *Isaiah 42:8*, and to *You* we make the distinction, that we call on no other god, but You Father; Deliver Us, and preserve us, and loose us from the lies of our minds, and the entanglements of Satan, and ALL his deception, Lord God, **in the** mighty **Name of** Your bloody sacrifice for the redemption of the entire world, Whose name is **the Word of God**, that the Angel told Mary His mother, that He shall be 'called' Jesus; in His Name to YOU do we pray. And THUS, WE GIVES OURSELVES TO YOUR WILL. DO whatever YOU Will with us, and we'll be made better for it, in Jesus' name. AMEN!

BIBLIOGRAPHY

Scripture. *See Copyright page*

Williams *(Weaver)*, Deon. K. *What Happened?* 2008. Library of Congress, Washington, D.C. Future/Past copyright, 2015. Unpublished.

Williams *(Weaver)*, Deon. K. *Friends.* 2014. As In Heaven, Inc., Georgia. Unpublished.

Author's Bio

Deon Kentell Williams was born having his mother's maiden name *Weaver*, and spent many years carrying that name, until having it changed to reflect his paternal bloodline! He is the son of Johnnie Lee Williams, Jr., and Shirley Ann (Weaver) Thurmond. As a fun fact, both his parent's share the same birthday (Month and Day), but 3 years apart!

Born in the USA, in the State of Georgia; city of Atlanta, *(where he was also raised)*. However, understanding that his heritage is that of *(one of)* the twelve tribes of Israel (God's chosen people historically)!
[The depictions on the movies, of Moses, Abraham; Jesus, are all lies!]

His maternal grandparents had a full hand in helping Deon become the person he has come to be. - This is mainly due to the reinforcement of integrity their lives and teachings taught, in addition to his mother's raising, and attendance of regular church services. However, it was around the age 9 or so, that he heard the voice of the Lord, for the first time himself.
(And received his call to preach the gospel of Christ).

At the age of 18 years, the young man encountered the LORD in a manner similar to that of before; *(hearing His voice unmistakably), but this time*, more life-branding and with much more detail! At this time, he heard the Lord speak to him that: He had called him 'into the Office of the prophet'; - something he was totally unaware of at the time and was taught immediately (by way of asking), what the function of being one of the LORD's *[true]* prophets are all about!
- [It is not what we've seen. Not even close!]

Author's Bio

Deon Williams submitted himself to the process, and at age 22, preached what's called, his "trial sermon"; = *a chance to see if the anointing and call of God is there as suspected by such spiritual leader(s) who noticed that it appeared to be this way; thus, providing a (first time preaching) opportunity.*

[Shortly after, the young vessel stepped away from the pulpit, choosing of his own doing and will, to prevent himself from being a hypocrite, (due to a sexual weakness he was experiencing with an induvial at the time). And it would be eleven years before he stepped foot in another pulpit and preached the gospel / word of God again in that format.]

– "Oh, time much well spent!" he says, growing in God.

On March 22, 2015, the minister became ordained as an Elder under the leadership of his pastor. *Bishop Dr. Wilfred Durrah, Jr.*

His educational background all stems from the Atlanta area, including his college matriculation, at the "illustrious" *Clark Atlanta University*; where he obtained a Bachelor of Religion/minor in Philosophy degree, and immediately begin to attend the seminarian master's degree program months later after graduation!

During his undergraduate experience, Deon started his first (music) company, *As In Heaven, Inc.*, in August of 2014, where the slogan is "God's Sound in the Earth". Two years later, in February 2016, *SOUL FOOD INTERNATIONAL MINISTRIES, Inc.,* was legally born. | www.SFIM.org.

Author's Bio

*The instructions were to lock the name in, but go no further, as the Lord told him also, *"You won't be ready to pastor until you're 36"*. - *being 35 at the time.* – And surely it was so! At age 36, with one month remaining before turning 37, SOUL FOOD INTERNATIONAL MINISTRIES' Inaugural service was launched, September 3, 2017.

You are invited to join us in worship!

After one (1) year and nine (9) months of serving in this capacity as pastor of this Founding ministry, the final and official decree was made of this sort, as Deon's bishop/pastor held the Official Pastoral Installation service for him on behalf of the *SFIMATL* flock, on June 23, 2019.

Beyond the invitations and engagements to minister at various churches locally, the prophet has ministered on *SpyTV* in Accra, Ghana, AFRICA, during his 2020 visit to the Motherland.

His authorship was prophesied openly by a visiting prophet to the church he attended from 2004 - 2012, sometime between 2006 or '7, or so, that Pastor Williams would write the books the theologians read from; *"a double theologian"* he was declared to be through prophecy! Also prior to, The *LORD* himself had been telling him, as a young man, to "write" for many years, but he didn't understand during those earlier years, that what he was to write would be books. There was uncertainly on what the Lord meant during those moments, frequently *throughout the years*. With there being nothing that 'he' deemed as pressing or specific, he put those things 'off' in disobedience; uncertain what sorts of writing he was being commanded to write in the first place. During that season, the word of the Lord, was simply to "write".

Author's Bio

He later understood that season to *"write"*, was not for books *(that would later come)*, but as an opportunity for sharpening and preparation of what would *(later)* be! Though he missed those moments in his youth, he understands the season for what it was now.

Let us hope that this won't be the last we hear of *Deon K. Williams* in this way, as an author, and continued friend of the truth.

For the Lord said so.

– WRITE!

www.ingramcontent.com/pod-product-compliance
Lightning Source LLC
Chambersburg PA
CBHW062038290426
44109CB00026B/2658